Your Face Is A Forest

Your Face Is A Forest

Rhyd Wildermuth

GODS&RADICALS PRESS

This work CC-BY-NA 2018
Rhyd Wildermuth

First Printing 2014

This is the second printing

ISBN: 978-0-9969877-8-3

Published by
GODS&RADICALS PRESS
PO BOX 11850
Olympia, WA, 98508

Direct all inquiries to the above address,
or email us at
Distro@ABeautifulResistance.com

Within

Into the Forest: 7
Knight of Cups, Knight of Wands: 9

Writings on the Wheel of the Year: 21
Now & Always Now 22
Hiding: 24
Eleutherios: 26
We See The Darkness: 31
Ceridwen's Gift: 34
The Light of the Earth: 37
Lady of the Forge: 39
Strings: 43

Wanderings: Journals From a Pilgrimage: 45
The Time Before You Leave: 47
Arrival: 50
Upon The Chemins: 53
Heather, Alder, Gorse: 58
At The Crossing of Three Rivers: 62
Penn Ar Breizh: 67
Walled Cities & Blind Saints: 71
Gates: 77
You: 81

In the Forest, A Dream: 87
Your Face Is A Forest: 88
Donnerlied: 90
Our Sister: 92
The Sword Pointed At The Heart: 93
The Sighted & The Blind: 95

Where They May Be Found: 101
Bran: 102
Arianrhod: 106
Cernunnos 109
Ceridwen: 112
Brighid: 115
Dionysos: 118
The Dead: 121

Spirits of Land: 125
Of Love & Land Spirits: 126
What I Know of a Creek 130
Under The Pavement The Forest: 133
The Garments of the Gods: 136
The Canticle of the Gates: 138

-To-

Everyone who's ever looked into the Abyss
And brought back light for the rest of us.

Into The Forest

This book is a collection of writing, which is a collection of words, which are lines and shapes corresponding to sounds which correspond to meaning, and that's where everything breaks down.

What's meaning mean? A word means something, and something means something else, and in between them is some thread of correspondence we call meaning. Someone means everything to me, but I don't know what that means except that it's pretty meaningful: *full of meaning*.

See what we get ourselves into?

One of the sorts of magic, from times we try to ignore, wove correspondences between things, cords and strands between above and below, this and that. They who did so were called mages, and wizards, and alchemists and sorcerers, but really, we might truthfully just call them weavers.

Bards, too, weave stories and song into tapestries, stringing together an image and another image into tableaux into which we are lost, or out of which we are found.

Words and magic aren't much different from each other. One thing is said and something becomes something else, someone is changed or killed or brought back to life. The correct words awakens a world or a dream, the artfully-spoken phrase crushes a soul or razes a forest.

Speaking of forests, this collection of words is the best I can do to lead you into one. You might get lost, or leave early, trip on a root or pick your way through brambles only to find it's only full of words, meaning nothing.
Or maybe you'll linger, see what I see when the wind shakes branches like laughter or rain soaks through leaf and frond into soil and stream. Maybe, even, you'll like it here, visit again, or even bring a friend.
It's all words, my tea-soaked threadings of one thing to another, weaving a forest from meaning, or meaning from a forest.

What's a forest mean?

What's meaning mean?

All I know is this: meaning is what connects you to others, connects us to the stars and the graves, to the light and soil, to the cities and the streams, to what we see and what we cannot see.

Meaning connects us to the world, meaning threads us to each other.

Meaning is another word for love.

20 October, 2014
Seattle, Washington

Your Face Is A Forest

Knight of Cups
Knight of Wands

Winter on the north shore of Boston is deep, a cold which clings so heavy it's hard not to imagine the entire world has retreated into frigid slumber. Though I'd been in South Florida my entire adolescence, loathing the thick humidity and searing heat of the dredged swamps, fantasizing about ice and chill winds, my first winter at college was brutal.

I'd fantasized about other things, too. I'd romanticized this part of my life, four years amongst old bricks, old streets, old cities, old words, reading old texts and learning profound truths as the snow fell, bitter but beautiful, outside my window. In Florida, skin sticky with sweat and salt, I'd dreamt of this sharp cold amongst books and thoughts–

And I'd dreamt about men.

The snow fell hard outside the windows. I was drinking shit hot cocoa, the sort that comes from white foil packets. So was Adam. We're sitting on the floor of the common room, the dry heater desiccating our throats as we play cards.

I'm trying not to stare at him while I talk. I don't remember what game we were playing, but I remember there being a Jack in my hand, and he'd just played a Jack, too. One was hearts, the other, clubs. For some reason, these cards made me try to tell him again.

"There's something wrong with me," I say.
He shakes his head, frustrated. "No, there isn't," he says, his gaze lifted from the cards to my eyes. I hate when he looks at me like this, I hate when he reassures me. I hate how much he cares and yet refuses to hear what I'm actually trying to say. So quick to reassure, to embrace, to distract me with laughter. I hate this all so much because I can't get him out of my head.
"Dude," I said. I used to say words like that. "I–I'm gay."

II.

I'd never said it that way before. I'd obscured it with metaphor, polite dancing about with words, prosaic allusions to a subject any of the men around me were too fucking dense to understand. I didn't want to use that word, or any other concrete description, and I regretted speaking it aloud once I'd said it. I felt I'd profaned the air around us, the frozen land outside. I'd profaned our friendship.
He was the hugging sort. Some men can be utterly homophobic and still embrace other men deeply, especially when Jesus is around somewhere. That name functions almost as a banishing ward, or a magical saining, cleansing brotherly friendship and touch from any potential sexual taint. So he's hugging me, and I'm crying. I don't want him to touch me, though that's all I've craved since I'd first met him. I don't want him to touch me this way, to hold me, to reassure me with his beautiful, deep voice that he'll help me fight.
I'd had a fantasy when I was younger. I'd crafted this image of man-love as two warriors going to battle together, holding each other close before marching to war, dragging each other off glorious, blood-soaked fields, mending each others wounds, fucking away each others' fear. And here's a man, holding me, tears in his eyes, offering to go to war with me, to fight alongside me, to wage battle against the evil we'd both seen.
But the fantasy's wrong. This is all wrong, and I am wrongest of all.
"You can beat this, don't worry."
I tried to restrain my anger at him, just as I'd always tried to restrain my lust. "Adam–I want to be gay."
His arms were gone. The stuffy over-heated warmth of the room suddenly gave way to the wintry chill, and now he was crying instead of me, grieving the loss of faith he thought he saw in the face of his best friend.

Your Face Is A Forest

III.

I'd met Adam a few years before, upon my second visit to Gordon College. I'd been selected for scholarship interviews and had flown on borrowed money from Naples, Florida to Massachusetts to attend a weekend barrage of interrogations about my faithfulness, intellectual discipline, and "leadership" skills.

Gordon is a Christian liberal-arts college. Most people haven't heard of it until recently, when its president signed a letter requesting exemption from all federal regulations prohibiting discrimination on the basis of orientation. Why'd I go there? I was Christian. Rather into it, at that time. I'd done a lot of praying, actually, as many of the people at the mega-church I attended in Florida were dubious about me going to a liberal-arts college. Everyone thought I'd go to seminary instead, expected me to go, and thought going to a "regular" college (despite it being Christian) would be a waste of my talents. Some people questioned the wisdom of me going to a college so close to Boston. Cities are full of sin and temptation, they'd reminded me. They were godless places, and many good Christian men had lost their way in Babylon.

They were on to something.

The time I went for my interview, my grandparents drove me there. My grandfather handed me 100 dollars and told me to find my way back to them in Hartford. No directions or suggestions, just a reminder to call if something went wrong and to "never count your money in front of people." After the interviews were done, I took my first train. I remember standing at the station, purchasing the ticket, feeling both a little scared but utterly exhilarated. I, 18 years old, having never lived in places with public transit, having dreamed since I was 12 of going to Europe, was taking a train by myself to a city.

I arrived in Boston pulsing with life and potential. At the station, I purchased my ticket for Hartford, and though I could have left immediately, I decided to postpone my return several hours. I'd never been to a city alone, nor one this big, and something seemed to call to me.

This is 1995. There's barely anything of an internet to speak of, mobile phones were confined to automobiles (car phones, they were called). If you're younger than me, the prospect of walking about a strange city and finding things to do without getting lost might not seem all that daunting. There are cell phones, after all, and mapping applications. You can look up whatever you want easily, find places that interest you and get back quickly by looking at a device.

You're missing out. Imagine: eighteen, alone, trembling with fear and lust for life, stumbling out of a train station onto strange streets with no idea what you're doing and no easy way of figuring out where you are?

There is nothing more fantastic.

I wandered the streets, looking into shops and offices, staring at brick and cobble, people and trees aimlessly, with no real intention except to see life and dream what I might be able to become.

And then I'm standing in a gay bookstore.

I didn't try to get there. I wasn't looking for one, but I'd wandered into it. Post- and greeting- cards with shirtless men, magazines, some wrapped in black plastic. Books about relationships and living with HIV, about home-making and Robert Maplethorpe, travel guides and art collections. Posters and rainbow flags on the wall, a large cardboard stand-up of Michelangelo's David.

I shouldn't have gone in, I knew. I shouldn't have been in there, so close to what I wrongly desired. The danger and transgression felt delicious, adrenaline and fear and excitement trilling through my body.

And then the shopkeeper said hello to me, so I fled.

IV.

I learned a few weeks later I'd been given the "A.J. Gordon Leadership Scholarship." It'd pay for half of my tuition and housing, and with need-grants I'd be able to attend without taking out huge loans. I needed only borrow $2000 each year, and work a bit during the school year to pay for books and other things.

While it was quite a relief to realize I'd be able to go to college, I was most excited about what it meant. The scholarship was something like a Fellows program. You got a special advisor and had meetings with the other recipients, all designed to cultivate leadership potential. Beyond expectations of high grades, one had to adhere to a particular version of the code of conduct which heavily emphasized influence on others behavior, conduct, and belief.

In other words, I became both a "leader" and a sort of enforcer. We were also required to take on officially-recognized leadership roles by the second year of college, and become increasingly influential each year until graduation.

This probably all sounds bizarre to some of you, but I was honored and excited. Some of this was the ego-stroking inherent in such recognition, but more of it was the potential to escape the poverty from which I'd come.

Your Face Is A Forest

I signed all the papers they gave me, tripping up only a little on the statements regarding homosexuality. I was to affirm in all I did that homosexuality was both a religious and cultural sin, against God's design and the proper functioning of societies. I should give no quarter to such sexual deviation in others, as I was to be a leader. And because I was a leader, the possibility that I might have had gay desires was inconceivable. Leaders couldn't be gay, because no leader would ever give in to such a thing.

I'd met Adam at those interviews for the scholarship. Lithe and muscular, his face angular, his smile fierce and disarming. He was strongly masculine in a gentle, dreamy way, his voice warm, deep, and kind.

One of the interviews was a group affair, thirty 18 year olds sitting in a circle while professors and administrative staff sat and observed. They'd given us note cards on which we were to order what we thought were the five most common reasons for going to college. Then, without any leading, we were all to discuss those reasons for an hour while the faculty watched, silently, taking notes.

They threw thirty strangers at each others' mercy and watched, like aristocrats at a Coliseum or social scientists at a homeless shelter.

It was a cruel and sadistic game, and one I'm very good at. Some people survive existence through money or strength, privilege or access. But I had none of that, so instead, like Oscar Wilde, I learned to dance through the realms of the social, weaving words and wit like magic into every encounter. I love people, and they're all I'd ever really had, so I'd become good at them.

I looked at Adam and said, "hey–what do you think?"

There'd been a lull in conversation. The first few who'd spoken at the beginning were the ones you learn to expect, the alphas, the men and women who'd been told all their life that they were powerful people, destined to lead. Each of them beautiful, with perfect teeth and great skin, talking with such authority that no one could possibly doubt their destiny. They spoke, and dominated, and everyone else sat quietly, beaten into submission. Those are the sorts who rule the world, clear-cut the forests, and crush indigenous revolts.

Adam looked back at me, his eyes alight. He wasn't quite ready to talk, had been under the spell of the inheritors of power. But he smiled, and fumbled with words, the first person to speak in answer to an invitation, rather than some notion of Divine Right.

I don't remember what he said. I could see the observers looking at each other and smiling, straining to see my name tag, scribbling quickly in their notebooks. I'd impressed them, I could tell. Perhaps I'd meant to, had known they'd be excited by someone widening the conversation, including others. Marks of leadership and all that trite shit.

Mostly, I just wanted to hear Adam talk. I wanted to watch his jaw move, see his slate eyes dart across the room nervously, regard his movements, his quickened breath and trilling body.

He spoke, and I regarded his charge across the grand circle of this absurd Coliseum, this strange battlefield, and I imagined one day dressing his wounds, wiping war-sweat from his face as we stared into each others eyes, trembling before our first awkward kiss.

Adam didn't get the scholarship, but I did.

V.

He said he'd go to war with me, but it was a battle I no longer wanted to fight.

I figured out I wanted men when I was eight years old. Then, I'd seen nothing wrong with such a desire. Sure, I'd known men were supposed to be with women, but an eight year old doesn't understand that the playful pre-sexual fantasies he engages actually mean anything to the rest of his life.

It didn't take long to figure out otherwise, though. An intolerant and uneducated ass of a father helps the process along pretty efficiently, as does all the policing by others through school. I got less pain and brutality on that matter from other boys.: it was the girls who enforced gender conformity with iron fists and sharpened nails, bitter words and social pogroms.

By thirteen, I'd become quite Christian. Youth groups are great places to sublimate homosexual desire, and Jesus is mannish enough that a creative pubescent boy can pour upon his deific form all manner of transmuted desire.

By eighteen, I'd spent 5 long years praying fiercely for God to take away my profane lust. I'd written to an "ex-gay" Christian counselor who replied with long letters about his success overcoming the homosexual lifestyle. He described in great detail his experiences in high school as a very masculine athlete who'd never come to grips with God's "purpose for men." He wrote about his descent into sin and depravity, sordid and tragic tales of sodomy with teammates on his football and soccer teams, truck stop blow jobs and drug-fueled group sex with men 30 years older than him.

I masturbated to his letters.

Your Face Is A Forest

VI.

After talking to a priest, I gave up trying to be straight.
Gordon College is non-denominational, but it's severely Protestant. Chapel attendance during the week was mandatory, but students were expected to attend a church of their choosing on Sundays off-campus.
I couldn't find one the first year. I'd occasionally go to the one Adam went to, but there was a lot of waving of hands and sometimes barking. He'd cry in divine ecstasy, passionate tears streaming down his face. I couldn't share the experience, as I'd already found the god of the Christians to be very distant.
Also, sitting next to him in tightly-packed pews–his muscled arms and legs pressing against mine–became unbearable.
A friend at the college, who'd been a critic of many of its policies, invited me to come with him to an Episcopal chapel. I declined repeatedly until I began to realise most of the people I liked went there. The commonalities in that group of friends were simple. We all liked reading, tea, and Europe, though most of us had never been. Also, most of us leaned politically left, though I'd just begun to work through my understanding of the larger world.
The priest there one day asked me to talk to her. I admired her, and she was the first priest I'd ever met, let alone talked to. She asked me if I had something I wanted to tell her. I didn't, but then I realized I did, and then blurted out, "I'm gay."
And she smiled and said, "good."
Before this, I'd fought so fiercely against my desires, my mind endlessly wrestling against my heart, that I hadn't known what it was like not to embrace a feeling. Admitting this to her felt amazing, and terrifying. The notion that I was "okay" had never occurred to me, though I'd always known fully the consequences of admitting my interior world to the external. I'd lose friends, certainly.
I'd also lose my scholarship.
Adam was the first person I'd told, and the most dangerous. He'd been my best friend, which, for a closeted gay man, is sometimes also a surrogate lover. It changes things, makes them distant, fearful.
We didn't talk much for weeks after that. I don't know whether the shame or the sorrow was greater. When I'd see him, I could see love in his eyes, but it was the love a man might feel for his brother who'd just be-

trayed his country. One thinks of the American Civil War, or Vichy France, brothers divided by ideology and nationalism, but not by affection.

I could feel the hurt in his words. He was a wounded knight, and though I tried to heal those wounds, we both knew my loyalty had changed. I'd forsaken my oaths to the kingdom of Heaven, and any embrace could be a prelude to blade-thrusts from behind.

I'd lost my greatest ally, my best friend, right at the beginning of war.

VII.

You can't be a A.J. Gordon Scholar as a homosexual.

I'd tentatively initiated conversations with those around me. A few were quick to shut down my trying with sharp words and silent stares; others were sympathetic but withdrawn. Only the new group of friends I'd made, the Episcopals, gave me any quarter, but most of them were fighting their own wars at the college, or intent on leaving at the first opportunity.

I told an Old Testament professor who seemed open-minded. She'd railed against young-earth creationism in her lectures, so she seemed certain to understand. She offered some sympathy, but stated that the prohibitions against Sodomy were clear.

"You can be celibate," she'd offered, helpfully, and gave me some articles about Catholic Mystics to read. "The desire isn't the problem, it's the action. If you never have homosexual sex, then you'll not have to worry."

It's funny that this relieved me. I told Adam this, and we became friends again. He vowed valiantly to stand with me on this. He'd guard my chastity, he said. He knelt when he said this, but not to me, to God.

Avoiding sex seemed a good resolution, and I got excited enough about this that I began to talk more openly with others about my desires for men. "It's okay," I would tell them. "Celibacy is devotion to God."

After talking so openly, it wasn't long until I had to answer questions from the advisers of the scholarship program. I'd overestimated my own skills of persuasion, the art with which I could move through the realms of the social. There's a theory that the social wit and skill of men like Oscar Wilde is how gay men survive in Western society. Our artful words becomes a weapon and also a key, opening to us the inner chambers of straight, white, male power.

Oscar Wilde didn't end up so well, either.

Your Face Is A Forest

VIII.

My conversations with the advisers went horribly. Worse, they'd been talking to each other about this, and were scrutinizing the rest of my behavior heavily, asking intrusive questions, checking up on me at odd times.

I became brutally depressed. The external pressure had become intense, but worse was the great sorrow of the apparent path before me. I could be a Christian and a leader and afford college if I never had sex with a man.

I was 20. I'd never had sex. And I could never have sex with a person I desired. Ever.

But hey–I had Adam to help me. He'd left a sweaty gym shirt in my room, and I slept with it at night. I'd visit his room when he wasn't there and put my face on his pillow to imagine myself close to him, taking in his scent. And Adam played piano. At night, he'd go to the chapel and play for hours. He'd invited me to come listen, and I did.

"Have you ever lain under a piano when someone's playing?" he asked.

I hadn't. He told me to, and I did.

I cried there. It's beautiful, the sound crashing into your physical form, untethering your soul. The notes course through your veins, ripping into muscle and mind. You are no more, only the music and the man playing the music.

I cried, but not just for the music. I cried for myself, for the whelm of desire under which I was drowning.

I got suicidal after this. Missed classes, got into arguments with my advisers. I worked as a Residential Counselor, and my supervisor, who'd been one of those kind, hippy Christians, became openly hostile to me.

I got so depressed I had to go to therapy. The college had contracted with local providers, and the therapist I went to prescribed me anti-depressants. She seemed suspended, restrained. Her face was sympathetic, but her words were always terse. I suspect she saw the easy answer to all of my problems, but could not tell me I should let myself be gay.

As part of the leadership requirements, I applied to become the editor of the college newspaper. I was quite excited, and the others interviewing me seemed quite positive. But one of my advisers of the scholarship program was in that interview, one to whom I'd confessed my homosexual desire and also my anti-depressant prescriptions.

"You suffer from depression," he said, in front of everyone. "And you're on medications. How do we know this won't affect your job performance?"

The answer I gave didn't assuage their sudden, collective doubts. I don't think any answer could have.

I didn't get the position, and I experienced similar doubts when I applied to become a Residential Counselor again. Only an appeal to one of the directors, who I knew went to an Episcopal church and seemed likely to be sympathetic, got me that position. I told him everything, the gay stuff, the depression, and particularly the fear about losing the scholarship.

I got that job, and he advised me not to tell anyone else that I was gay. I'm no good at shutting up, though.

IX.

The anti-depressants were horrible, pulling from me all my creativity and the last dregs of desire for life left in my spirit. To get off of them meant possible suicide, but to stay on them meant living death. I stopped taking them and began to stare at my despair. This isn't easy, isn't fun. Everything I was inclined towards a kind of desire, while everything around me walled such lust away.

Most of my friends had become distant. I was a Residential Counselor, but the other guys on my floor had lost respect for me once they'd heard I was gay. Most of them, jocks, would come into my room shirtless in their loose boxers or torn gym shorts to talk about Jesus or girls or how difficult college was. That stopped once they began to understand what might have been going on in my head. Not seeing their ripped bodies and experiencing their playful banter actually took some pressure off, but the ostracization was horrible.

But worst of all, Adam was never quite the same.

This self-avowed champion of my sublimated sexuality, my monastic, celibate destiny, had a girlfriend. The worst times were when she visited and he'd disappear from my existence for days. They tried to include me sometimes, inviting me to the beach with them towards the end of the school year. I went once, and I vowed never to put myself through such torment again. Their relationship looked like a film, the final, beautiful moments of resolution in a romantic comedy.

"I can't do this," I told him. "I'm gay. I'm going to be gay."

That look again, those tears. "No—you said…"

I shook my head. I was angry, tired of being mired, trapped, restrained. Fire coursed through me, and I wanted to burn everything around me.

Your Face Is A Forest

I told him I wanted to love, too. I would not live the rest of my life suspended, restrained, devoted to a god who'd demand that I live forever without desire.
"You'll lose your scholarship," he warned me. He wasn't angry now, but afraid for me. Care and love soaked his words, reforged his face.
I went to an administrator. I'd heard she might be tolerant, maybe she'd help. I explained everything to her, as best as I understood it.
"So, if I'm gay, I'll lose this scholarship?"
She nodded and stiffened.
"Uh, I'm gay, so I'll lose this scholarship, I guess."
She nodded.
"I can't afford to go here otherwise."
"You'd like to withdraw, then." It wasn't a question. She handed me the forms I needed, and I left the office, and that was it.
The administrative building where I'd first interviewed, where I'd charmed the advisors for that scholarship, and where I signed my withdrawal papers is a reconstructed medieval Irish castle, built from stone imported across the sea. It was hard not to think of kings and knights when you looked at it.
I walked in there a student. I left a drop-out, a failure, and a fag.
And then the rest of my life began.

X.

In Tarot, the Jack of Hearts is the Knight of Cups, the Grail Knight. He's the sensitive dreamer, the seductive poet, the romantic fool.
The Jack of Clubs is the Knight of Wands, the revolutionary, the radical, the liberator. Charming and inconstant, the black-clad anarchist who lights a fire to start an insurrection and is gone.
The first is water, the other fire, and between them, I think--desire.
I saw Adam a few years after leaving college. He'd gotten married to a different woman after getting jilted by his fiancée. He seemed happy with his life, and unhappy with me. I'd visited him on my way to somewhere else, a brief stop, but in that short time he understood that I was someone else.
We were brothers, staring at each other in recognition and confusion across a trench. He'd become more Christian, I'd become a Pagan. I'd fucked men, his wife was expecting a child. I was an Anarchist, he'd become Libertarian.

Knight of Cups, Knight of Wands

"Why do you have to throw that in my face?" he demanded. I'd made him angry, referring to something about a lover I'd been with.

My words were a shot across the line, an attack, an assault in a battle I didn't want to join.

"Why do I have to hide that from you?" I asked.

And there was nothing else to say. We stood there, swords drawn, ready to wound without knowing why, brothers, reluctant warriors ready to slay.

Instead, we turned and walked away, knights of our respective domains retreating from each other in silent truce. That game of cards had ended when I played my Jack, or when he played his. I do not remember which one he played, or which one I played.

And I do not think either of us won.

Writings On The Wheel Of The Year

In several Pagan traditions, the four solar holidays (two solstices, two equinoxes) and the four 'cross-quarter' days (roughly February 1st, May 1st, August 1st, and November 1st) are celebrated as holy-days. Some peoples see these days as linking to the patterns of the earth and the stars, or to the seasons, or to cycles of human life; others suspect something even deeper. In America, only Samhain (Halloween) and Beltane (May-Day) have any lingering celebration; the first a night of masks and trickery, the second a day of masks and protests.

There are "Mysteries" to be found in celebrating these eight days, and the following pieces were the results of my attempts to dream through them, watching the threads of meaning weave about my life in accordance to their hidden currents.

Now & Always Now
(Beltane)

He stands before a gaping wound in the earth. Sun beats down, waiting,
beating with the drums,
waiting.

Women and men heft an elder upon shoulders, struggling,
sweat, strain, hope,
waiting.

At the wound, at the center,
the elder, its life given,
waits to fill, waits to heal.

A man doesn't know why, doesn't ask why.
Holds a rod of wood, breath streaming through it,
wind from flesh resonating, making wood sing,
waiting.

Across the abyss that waits,
waits to be repaired, the wound that waits to be healed

Your Face Is A Forest

as the drums wait, beating,
as the women and men heft and struggle,
waiting, is a woman,
waiting.

She wields jade, a bowl. It sings in her hand.
She stares across the pit at the man, the man who stares at her.

And they are suddenly one, one with those who carry weight
of life upon shoulders, weight of tree hefted, one with
those who wait between the beat of drum, one with the waiting.

The man plays, the woman plays, the drums play.
Wails.
Shouts, a chant
all is about to break all to be made whole.

The man sees the woman, he sees other women, he sees other men, men
he has loved, men he loves, men who loved and love men he has loved
and loves and will love, men he hopes to love.
He sees sweat on a beautiful brow,
he sees eyes from a mountain, he sees
eyes seeing something distant, something he wishes to see,
something he thinks he will one day see, maybe with those same eyes.

And then all is broken, all is made whole,
the pole is raised, the rift is healed, the hole is filled,
and all is suddenly one, all is suddenly new, all is suddenly now again,
now and always again,
now and always now.

And there is no longer any waiting.

Hiding (Midsummer)

Suspended over a river of concrete the edge of a forest lingered, just off the edge of my vision. All my visions seem like this, just off the edge of sight, the peripheral within the liminal, only-there in the place one's unclosed eyes go when one looks away.

He stood there before the forest-that-wasn't there, massive, what man desires in himself, what man strives to become, what man runs in terror from. Frightening in his beauty, his virility, and his indifference. Ancient forest embodied, where no longer forest stands.

Later, I stood in the middle of revelers, watching, hearing thunder in my body, not in my ears, watching.

Words in song, song in screams, screams forming words which evoked, invoked, lamented arrogance, lamented destruction. I could not tear my eyes from the ringed-tree suspended from his neck, nor my mind from the unveiled invocations, nor the figure of the forest outside.

The moment of the sun's height. A circle, strangers, fumbling with pages. Then the sky fell away, though the Great Light lingered, and beyond the encircled figures (nimbused in this other world in white and yellow) the trees and beyond the trees the stars. The crown raised, the sword heft, another union accomplished both here and always, a thousand times over, a

Your Face Is A Forest

thousand times at once. Ancients watched with us, stag, hawk, bear and salmon saluted, and then the unwound ring and snacks.

Crossing the bridge away from that place another vision, warm gold across vast fields, but then the sun's red was fire, and the field burned, and I looked away.

They hide, just as we do. We'd patent their genes if they had bodies we could imprison, we'd sell them vapid plastic. They hide, we hide.

We hide from each other. I've known men who hide their glances behind lenses and then note their interest later in unread forums. Those who look and look away, down, and search the phone in their hand to divine another's preferences, occupation, length.

We hide behind screens, yes, but we hide behind masks, too. I know a man whose dark profundity is hidden behind manic joy. Another veils deep awareness with frivolity. A third whose radiant beauty is cloistered by diminished presence, a fourth who's cached his exalted brilliance inside apparent stupidity.

We hide behind masks, and we hide behind mirrors, we hide from each other and we hide from ourselves.

It is no surprise they hide from us, but I have learned, lately, they are not hiding very well. They are only barely out of sight, it seems, lingering like the forest just beyond the concrete, the sea below the pavement, the birdsong and laughter heard but unseen.

It is no wonder, I understand, that we do not see them. We can barely look at each other.

Some believe the gods and the spirits are only within us, but this is the spell of the screen, the veil, the mirror.

To see what is hiding, looking away must become a way of looking at, an unmirrored gaze.

In-between the glance and the glance, the gaze and the regard, is the Other, hidden, like our selves, like each other, hiding in plain sight.

Eleutherios
(Lughnasadh)

Bale'corn will soon die.
                    Do not ask Them if you would not know.

    Earlier under the willow, reading. How it was once seen, how we once thought. Replace confused words of desire from one with the archaic searchers of desire from people gone into the dark.
    Later, under a pine.
    What the tree asks, I do. My book, my thoughts, back against trunk, leaning against desire known in a different time.

Brigidh
                    Do not look there if you would not leave.

    In a cold house I was the only hearth, and She at it, laughing. Not smothered, only smouldered,
    And here again the candles, here again the flame.

    At Imbolc, I left the tower, the web, the loom, after the mirror cracked, walked through the gate to the forests and saw there a satyr.

Your Face Is A Forest

"This is a tree. This is oxalis," he said, then fed me from blue-blossomed vines a nectar. "This stone calms," he said. "This stone heals. This is my fur," he said, "and this is my heart beneath it."
At Eiler, the first turning of the path we parted with oaths.
"I can hear you from there," he said.
Under the pine, my back against the only thing strong enough, he said "I can hear you from here," and I smiled and rubbed my neck against bark.

Brân

Do not play to Them if you would not be heard.
John Barleycorn should die.

Wooden shield, sustainer of armies.
I played for him on an island, dark-winged birds wheeling.
I thought they were birch, until I knew they were Alder.
Elk-tooth through the forest, in my hand, moss from one Grandmother to another.
Stag, moss, Alder.
I open a bottle of wine and leave it out for him, whom I chided, but I hold close to the branch he gave me.

Arianrhod

Do not ask if you would not have Them give.
Do not ask if you would not have Them take.

At Beltane I stared into her sky. The stars wheel, and there, her crown, her citadel, where I lost a name and took another.
He has been called inconstant, yet hanged her circle of light for us then to see.
She crossed over sea, away from him, over her father's threshold.
There gave birth, there gave back to the sea,
There took all away from the other to let him make himself.
I have been in her court, though I did not know her.
I have been in her court, but I did not know myself.

An old woman under a willow breaks off a branch for her dog.
A young girl swings from a Birch, and I know it will break, too.

Fallen branch, wet into a pool of stars, water dripping like bells.

"I am the Queen of Witches," she says. Blue reflected in silver, her owl. "You would know him?" she asks.

"Take this to protect from your own love, this to remember what you try to forget."

He loved her. I did not understand this until I saw the stars through needled branches and felt his desire, pining.

Ceridwen

> Do not offer your hand if you
> would not have it taken.
> Do not seek life if you would not
> know the death which gives it shape.
> Do not seek light if you would not
> know the darkness which gives it birth

Jean Saint Pépin serait mort.

I walked between houses which did not know me, under a scythe moon which would blood me. Black-iron pot in my small rucksack, blackest of darknesses in my heart.

Her hideous son. Towers of glass, a recipe-book, a year of stirring. The boy, he did not steal it, but you cannot know life if you will not know death.

There, his seed. There the death. There, then, the birth.

"You would know him?" She laughs. "I will show you his death."

The Mothers

> Don't.
> Just don't, unless you mean it.

I laid against him. Blood drawn from thorn of holly feeds pining roots. "Quiet," he says, "they are greater than I."

They demand, and I plead. More blood, but I only have enough for myself. More blood until flesh is drained. It was only three drops, the boy had said, and yet this was enough, they had said.

Your Face Is A Forest

But they spin and weave and cut, and so do I.

"You have my blood," I say. Winged water-wisps pierce my skin. "Others feed on their blood," I say, "which is mine, for they have stolen it too. 'Three drops is enough,' you said, but my blood will now run forever in streams of flesh-eaten-flesh."
"True," they say, and laugh, and the threads are woven again.

Dionysos

Ask.
By the pine where ale poured deep,
just before the dance of desire–
ask about that dance.
Ask about those howls to the stars in his forests.
Ask as a friend and get an answer,
as a child and get the truth.

Clad in green, with his hair around his eyes.

Pine. I ask.

In the place where we first met his arms are suddenly around me. He's not there, but he is behind me anyway. I did not know he was so tall.
"Tell yourself what I tell you," he says. "Remind yourself in the morning." "And look," he says. "That man there knows me. He tends my shrine, he dances my dance. Use your words, like you did with Them when I told you to shut up and listen."
I stumble, wheel around him like her stars, throw myself into the dark roiling abyss, and surprise myself with my words. They're the same words I'd tell myself. "You already know this," I say, "but you're fucking beautiful."

In the morning, I try to piece it back together. Hours of words by the hearth, but weren't we in a forest of pine? There was dancing, but we were both still. Satyrs laughed and fucked and howled at her moon, at her crown, by her springs, but we were still.
In the morning, I wake and look at the wand of alder, the mug of tea. There was a dance, and there's proof, but it was from another time. There's the chalice with silvered vines, the wine.

Writings on the Wheel Of The Year

"Eleutherios," I'd said. And thunderer, and the howls are still here.

John Balleycorn'll die,
his seed consumed,
and me with it.

I know this story.

I am this story.

Again and-

We See The Darkness (Mabon)

I said to a friend, "we see the darkness."

    We all see the darkness. It's there, it lingers, it breathes just outside the light. It shapes, it shadows.
    I walked through a dark forest without light and saw the other light. It is like ours, but without sun. It is like the moon, but without a face.

I said to a friend, "we see the darkness, and some go in."

    Others don't. I understand, but this is not enough.
    I walked again through a dark forest with a taper. It melts, burns the hand that shields the fragile flame. It illuminates even less than you'd expect, except when steps cease. And outside the circle of light? Darkness, which is deeper.

"We see the darkness, and some go in.
It is the abyss."

Writings on the Wheel Of The Year

Tired? He fled for so long. There could be no blame. Chased through sky and forests, rivers, wars, destruction. Sea breaking upon land. Axe in hand.
  No.
The last trick, final cunning, the last place he'd be found? Glinting against sun, wind through pinions. Before thrones, bound in prison. Where else could he hide?
  No. I wasn't hiding.

I said to a friend, "We see the darkness, and some go in.
It is the abyss.
We have to find out what is there,
to find where the meaning leaks out."

Our faces hold the light of others who are gone.
Our faces become lined with shadow in their absence.

A final stand, then? Being chased so long, fatigue turned to rage, like the ermine seen by Breton kings just as the conquerors rolled in to slaughter. Turned like the ermine, flattened under wheel, a final, futile gesture to inspire those who'd remain?
  No. That would have been futile, as you say.

I said to a friend, "We see the darkness, and some go in.
It is the abyss.
We have to find out what is there, to find out if there is meaning.
And we see only the abyss.
And some go mad.
And some never return.
And some—"

I don't know, then. Why?

The hunted hunts.
There is no hunt without the hunted.
There is no hunt without the hunter.
I wanted to see how much She wanted me.

Your Face Is A Forest

"And some," I said,
"come back wielding light against that darkness.
Seeing nothing, we bring back fire,
we light lamps, candles, torches.
We hold light that isn't ours,
as how else would anyone else see?"

    Hold a candle in a dark forest and walk into the trees.
    The wax burns your hand, but it cools.
    The light illuminates little as you walk.
    And don't imagine for a second
    that the candle is for you,
    but hold it anyway,
    because something is looking for you.

Ceridwen's Gift
(Samhain)

Death. Speak the word with voice, not just your mind. Look upon it. Play with it.
It is to be feared less than Life.

Some believe in only one god, a promise of life which comes after life, which defeats Death, as if they would also defeat Life. Some believe in no gods, and no life after life, no life after death, only death and the mystery of Life. I believe in gods. I've been called by One who means Death: Death, which is Life, which is again Death then Life.

Her cauldron is never still.

Death is coming for a matriarch, and this is a great sorrow. But in her face I saw the crone look out, reminding me to tend Her cauldron.
Death came for a patriarch, a life lived in suspension, in expectation of a peaceful life after work. The tending was done before he'd finished, before he'd finally lived.
This was his lesson to me. This is Her lesson to us.

Your Face Is A Forest

She drowns children, She calls from the sea which is the womb of all life. We crawled aeons before from Her salt tears to the rim of Her cauldron. Some of us crawl back into the ocean, summoned or pulled or chased.

Death comes for others so quickly, so close to what seemed the dawn that we rage.
We foam like Her waves, we scream at and through Her moon.
We try to pull it down to understand, we try to blot it out, and all the while, we stir Her cauldron.

Death will come for me some day, but this is less hard than what comes between Death.

Death is the water of life.

It is our food, fed upon life cut down with scythes or blade, ripped from earth and plucked from branch.
It clothes us in skin no longer covering flesh, it warms us by mirthful hearths.
It runs our machines which run us into other lands, which will one day run us under a dying earth.

There is no sense to Death, except as the shape, the shadow, and the light of Life.

How can we see Life without its end?
How can we whet desire without its loss?

In love is Death.

What was, goes away, dies, clears for new life.

In Death is love, and this is not strange–
But beautiful, Her pale face
gazing upon the life she birthed with death,
the life she fed,
life cradled in her crescent arms,
her silvered sharpened scythe.

Writings on the Wheel Of The Year

Death and Life dance in Her cauldron
and I think
Life is the greater Mystery.

Do not shun Her gift.

Live.

The Light of the Earth
(Winter Solstice)

The Welsh Druid tradition calls the midwinter solstice Alban Arthan, the "Light of the Earth." The sun shines upon us, illuminating our darkness. But there is another light, what remains when there is no other light, the light that is within us when all other brightness is stripped away.

A year ago, during a heavy downpour, I put on my black hooded-sweatshirt, hefted my rucksack upon my back, and stepped out into a cold night, walking away from my home and the man who had been my lover for three years. I have known no darker night than that one. I wasn't "kicked out;" rather, I'd made the decision that, since he and I were "over" and he had nowhere else to go at the moment, I would leave for awhile. I don't know if it was selfless or selfish, whether there could have been something that might have been said that could have undone the end. Maybe, but that no longer matters.

I spent the next few weeks elsewhere, returning to my house when my former lover was not home in order to make him a Black Forest Cherry-cake for his birthday, as I'd promised and it made no sense to reneg on this. I remember attempting to frost it through tears, and then he arrived, and we both tried to fix the mess I'd made of the chocolate whipped-cream frosting.

There is no bitterness here.
Sometimes things don't work, no matter how much effort you put into them. Sometimes things just are not good, and the good you try to make of it becomes an increasing sorrow, something which exhausts you, ebbs from you both your strength and your capacity for joy.
Into that cold, rainy night I tread, having no idea what had just happened, nor any clue what was about to. I'd had dreams before this time which had panicked me so much their brilliance brought me anguish.
A woman staring at me in reflection, her glance both stern yet patient, waiting for me to figure out something, to listen to her, to find out what it was she was trying to tell me.
And another dream, myself in a great host of people waiting at a gate. I needed only know a name to enter in, but I did not know that name. A rain had begun to fall, everyone was entering, but I could not yet.
Someone in the throng took pity on me, noted my confusion. "I don't know how to get in. What's the passcode?" He smiled, nodding with the sort of kind understanding that makes you immediately trust a man. "Oh. It's Brighid. You can tell by the way the rain is falling, and what is between the rain."
It rained for weeks. One night I stood alone in a park at 3am, crying, talking to myself, composing what I'd say to my former lover if I could. The words wove a story I didn't know to tell myself yet, one I'd spend the next 12 months attempting to tell.
Sometimes, I think, I had forgotten about that other light. When the world is bright, all becomes hued in vivid color even as the shadows lengthen. The glory of the sun defines us, delineates us more sharply from others. But in the darkness, in that other light, all is shadow. We are less different from the earth, less different from each other when undressed by silence and stillness. Shapes merge, coalesce, become all one in our unseeing. But we are still there, and there is the light of the earth, of us, of me.
A year ago, all was sorrow. There's been little sorrow since, except that I maybe hadn't noticed. One becomes so accustomed to struggle, so fortified against pain, so strongly defended against each new onslaught that one forgets why we struggled in the first place, what was hoped for at the end of the defenses. I say "one," but I really mean "me."
That gate I thought I was trying to enter? It was actually the gate out.
That darkness in the middle of winter? It's actually the light of the earth.

Lady of the Forge (Imbolc)

They seem to litter in their scattered array, bits, stubs, burnt-out ends. Drippings cascading down ledges and stilled, icicles without chill. Splashed upon the wooden floor and then frozen by the cold we call comfortable.

They were all once light and a bit of warmth; they are now only fragments, the residue of memory, dreams misshapen, pooled, lumpen in sconces, soaked into blue cloth upon an altar, fused into the grain of a wooden box.

And Brighid tosses more fuel upon her hearth, and laughs.

The Guardian of the Tower

Here are the remains of pillars.

When I saw Brân, his great black cloak rippled in an unseen wind, his powerful form straddling a Breton valley between the River of Alder and the sea. But the cloak fled from his body, a myriad of ravens having stripped from him his flesh sinew and skin, leaving only great white pillars of bone, the foundation of a temple and a tower. I do not yet know where his head lies.

These gave light for days which became months and years. Here, the garden, here the balcony overlooking a lake, here the lake walled by the roots of mountains. Here the work that gave meaning. Here, the long loves, the friends and men and cities, all burnt out, blackened fragments of wick and ash.

These, we can use.

The Harvester

These were once tapers.

Stubs fused into holders. I never trim the wicks, huh? These burned too quickly, flaring and sputtering in the draughts. These gave light at dinner, or when I wrote. When a lover and I shared another, or when I shared my home to great throngs of friends and strangers.

These also I burned in sorrow, staring long into their flames in hope of solace, against a darkness within when the light without had grown so very dim. When he told me he no longer loved me, or when I told him I no longer did. When I was so poor I berated a lover for the extravagance of a pear, or so exhausted I broke my bagpipes when I collapsed on them.

The tiny bit ends I lit when there was so little left for me, or so little left of me. Tiny tapers, 5 for a dollar at the apothecary, enough light for a remembrance of hope.

Here, too, the ones which burned wrong, or melted too fast, the ones that caught other things in their flame and molten wax. This one when I, caught up in the joy of life and trust in the world, was raped.

This other one when I tried to give love and found it met with utter hatred. These here when an idea of what the world might become was crushed by the cynicism of others or the long grinding-down of the body against the weight of others' demands.

And these?

Ah. These are the ones I made wrong. Here, the wick was too thick, the wax too quickly consumed against the brilliance of the flame. Others, here, the opposite. Braided cord which drowned in the molten well. These didn't become what they should, didn't become what they could. The lit journal, the move to Europe, the plans to return to school. The unfinished manuscripts, the medieval band. Misforged. Failures.

Your Face Is A Forest

So much wax left over. Good.
These we can especially use.

I hadn't expected, you know, to find Ceridwen's death-face to be so kind.

The Crown of the North
These other ones?

The ones I like a lot!
Look, here—I made this one. See how the colors blend into each other? Greens and blues fading together into whites. The colors fade into each other like the forest into the sky reflected in a pool, like when I noticed Arianrhod. Remember? You were there too, certainly. And remember how I'd always stare at my reflection in puddles of water on stone so to see the sky above me, but in that strange light that isn't from the sun? And know there was something more?
And these over here, I made for others. I haven't sent them yet. Look! This one from the wax of bees, and this other one scented with vetiver. Remember when I used to grow vetiver? Remember when I had it imported and kept one inside every year so that it would survive the winter and I could separate its roots come spring, come every February when the world turns warmer and all of life begins to awaken again?
Remember how all those new things which birth themselves in the darkness of winter begin to move under the earth? And so many candles like this, because it's been winter and this is when it's easiest to make them. I'll light them the next time I'm with a lover, or when I host friends, or even when I feel sorrow again. All these I haven't used yet, because they're for later, or for others. So much hope!

We should use one of these, too.

When I was child, a man came from the stars and had me read a book. I'd thought he was an astronaut until he brought me inside and he was dressed like a monk, and the book was like none I've ever seen.
Every night for over a week I read from it until I finished and he said he could go back to the stars. I've never seen him again, but I think he was there in castle where I got my name, and I didn't realize until recently whose stars he came from and whose castle I'd been in.

Writings on the Wheel Of The Year

The Lady of Fires and Rain

Lady of the hearth. Lady of the springs. Lady of the forge. Lady of the light.

I remember her beckoning. She waited for me to notice (and how long had she waited? So many years, wasted like so much unspent wax, like the stubs and ends and drippings of candles, scattered about my home, about my life).

"It's Brighid," the man had said, laughing. We'd all gathered outside a gate, and I couldn't see what was beyond. People from all nations, women in cloaks and shawls, men in rough clothes and colored garb. So few drest richly it makes me wonder still, but all were beautiful.

I'd asked him what word I needed to know to enter. His face was so kind, full of a pleased mirth. "It's Brighid," he'd said, so much life in his voice. A light rain, like that of late spring had begun to fall. "See the way it's falling?" he asked. "You can tell it's her by the way it falls, and by what's in-between the rain."

From under the earth rain springs upward. From above us light torrents down upon us.

Here is something new, made from all that was old. In the heart of the hearth I'll gather these bit-ends of lights that were, and into it I'll add what might be. In the heat of her forge what was becomes what can be, what could have been becomes what should be.

She does not forge from nothing. All that was becomes what is and will be. We inhabit the past even as we live in the present and create the future.

In her reforging is her poetry, and in her poetry is her love, springing from the earth, falling with and in the rain and what is in-between that rain, and she tosses more fuel upon her hearth, and laughs.

Strings
(Ostara)

It isn't untrue to say my life is composed of strings. Cords of cotton and nylon to bind together my affects, to blouse the cuffs of my pants over boots bound to feet by laces. Thin leather strips to close cloth bags holding cards, wooden tiles marked with archaic letters, thicker pouches of stones and coins corded shut by suede.

There are the heavier ropes, braided hemp woven through the grommets of my rucksack, the strong thick leather of my belt, the suspenders crafted for me years ago by a lover. The thick lengths of tree fiber, grown together, which support the weight of my body upon a chair, a bed, across a floor.

Then, the thinner strings. The copper wire twined around the wand of Alder, binding to it feather of raven and crystal of earth. That same wire ties together the braid in my beard, itself composed of myriad thin strands of hair which also covers much of my body. The threads–oh, the threads! Filament of plant and animal fiber woven together into cloth to cover my flesh where hair and nudity are insufficient or unaccepted. Thicker fabrics cover me when I sleep, shade out the light from my room in the morning, dry my skin after showers.

Writings on the Wheel Of The Year

Also, those newer of connections, the other wires, channelling within them like veins and nerves below flesh amberic currents and signals between artifice and signal, generation and illumination.

Strings and wires and cords bind me and embrace me and restrain me, but they are not mine alone.

There are other filaments, unseen but always felt, invisible but ever-present. Some tie you to me, thoughts and dreams, laughter and hatred, what is shared and what is feared. I meet you and we are tethered, sometimes anchored, sometimes set aloft like connected balloons slipping from the hands of children into the endlessness of sky. Some tie me to you, affection or dislike, duty or admiration, care or casualty, love or loss. Some are like chains which weigh upon the soul, but many others like long stitches which keep us together.

Not just in present, either. There are the threads of fate woven into my form and existence at birth and from even before, the tugging strong rope of destiny unfolding, and all the myriad unfollowed threads of stories and sorrows, possibilities and failures still loose.

I've heard existence spoken of as a web, but I have never quite felt this true. Webs are spun to constrict and trap, to bind and kill. A broken strand does not destroy it. Its patterns can be predicted, its geometry assured.

No.

Rather, then, a tapestry, woven from time and the self, of threads countless and coloured, and each strand is you, and you, and you, and some of them are me.

We do not weave alone, and we are not the only ones at the loom. What are we weaving, we whose cords are cut at the end of life, who become respun into new threads?

Some threads are the gods. And this is a thing I do not understand, but from which I cannot look away: the gods seem almost the pattern we learn to weave, but I do not know how, nor do I know why. And I do not know why they weave with us, and why we weave with them.

I hope one day to find out.

Wanderings: Journals from a Pilgrimage

From the Sixth of September to the tenth of October, 2013, I traveled alone through Northwest France (Brittany) and Germany on Pilgrimage.

A bit of the story as to why I did this is in my public travel journals, which follow. The rest of the story is still unfolding, the dreams, visions, and voices from my journey still resounding.

If you are told to leave everything you have, your home and job and life, to stuff what you can into a rucksack, purchase a trip to some other land to go see the things which appear to you in dream, it's hardly sane to do so.

But I think you should, anyway.

The Time Before You Leave

3 September (Seattle)

My higher-mind functions are a bit off currently. I've been thinking about this as it relates to the binary thinking of sane/mad, spiritual/mundane. The last couple of days at work I wrote extensively in my spare moments, which were few as there were people screaming (always people screaming) and it was my last continuous access to both a computer and a printer.

The essay I was trying to write was regarding Madness and Belief. If I ever finish it, I'll post it. Suffice for now to say that I've been working on a conceptual framework and a theory as to why there was such an initial resistance within my mind when I started encountering the Other.

This statement isn't completely true–the resistance was more social than mental: that is, I more needed to check with others (constantly) that what I was seeing, sensing, hearing, dreaming and feeling did not qualify as madness, regardless of how otherwise quite well-trained I am in recognising the signs of mental imbalance in others.

Last night was my final shift as a low-level, underpaid social worker for a homelessness agency. Not altogether bad, I guess, though I'm utterly re-

Your Face Is A Forest

lieved to be free of it. One of the clients dressed in drag and prophesied for me (a strange experience in itself, which goes back to my attempts to find the precise line between the insane and the spiritually-aware): I am to have sex on the steps of a cathedral, and if I do not wish to take a plane, the woman who comes down from the stars will take me up, he said. Another particularly mad client told me that, instead of going to France, I should go to Florida.

Speaking of Florida (strange woman), I have an extensive contingency plan in case I find myself not staying in Europe. This involves hitting much of the east coast and then crashing with my sister in south Florida for awhile until–well, I can barely plan a week ahead, so such a question is useless to ask.

The possibility of staying has come up a few times in other's readings of my situation, though my own divinations make it rather clear I'm to return for some reason. I've been joking it will be with an army.

I washed my tent today.

I went to a Radical Faerie gathering in Beltaine, and because I was perhaps the only fag who went for the Pagan part of the Pagan-sex aspect of the gathering, the forest gave me an STD anyway: poison oak. I don't think I've mentioned this to many, but I think I laid a towel down on a patch of it and then dried my entire body after an open shower in a field. *I dried my entire body.*

The doctor, otherwise professional, could not stop cringing and laughing sympathetically when he saw how incredibly large certain areas had become.

So, on the off-chance some of the oil from the plant remains in the tent, I washed it. Simultaneously sorting through the stuff I intend to take. I am stubbornly leering at my journals, willing them to become a bit lighter, as I refuse to not take every one of them.

4 September (Seattle)

I packed my bag and everything fits. I can say with almost complete confidence that I'm not forgetting anything, that everything I need will be inside that bag. If all goes well, it might even make it to Europe with me.

I've been really into the idea of story for most of the last decade, but it's taken on a new meaning and power for me since beginning Druidry. The first grade, the Bardic grade, focuses much on learning the uses of story, the

Wanderings

hidden meanings woven into certain sacred myths, and the stories that can be told about the mundane which infuse the world with the existence of the Other.

And the last couple of weeks have seemed much about completing stories, ending them, or at least closing circles of the worlds contained within that story so that its unwoven threads do not snag or fray. Particularly as I am leaving this city and have no intentions of returning, these stories, which are also the stuff of my dreams, the material of my meaning, have each paraded themselves before me as if to say, "write my ending."

The psychological way of putting this is "getting closure." I dislike the sterility of the term, but it's another useful way of understanding what I mean.

I've had two deep, profound loves while in Seattle. I've had many loves, each of them beautiful and meaningful, but the ones where you decide to write your story with another, when two people decide not just to love and fuck and care for each other but to co-create their worlds–that is what I mean by deep, profound love, and of these I have two.

The most recent one ended last winter, and it's been a little difficult to narrate that story into completion and, more so, narrate that story into my life now without letting the sadness of its ending stain its threads.

Also, funny thing about me that I've recently recognised–the ideas of love lasting forever and the notion of a lover being "enough" for one (that is, monogamy) have always held intense sway over my heart, simultaneous to me being quite the prophet of open-relationships and knowing that all things must end for them to have ever begun.

A lover isn't just a partner or a friend, he's a fucking world, a dream incarnate, a canvas upon which you paint your desires, a spring from which you draw your inspiration, a wind which carries upon it hope. The unraveling of that kind of love is always difficult, and it's even harder to write the ending of those stories than any other.

The most recent lover and I met for a final time last night and made dinner together like we used to, ending it with hot cocoa. It was an old pattern, soaked in meaning, but fraught with nothing except kind recollection. And we both told each other I think what was most necessary to hear–we shall remember the other always in love, with no hurt or sorrow or "what if," just in love.

Your Face Is A Forest

The previous lover, a wild, dream-filled 9 year affair, reminded me in an email yesterday that I will be leaving for France very close to the time when he and I returned from France roughly 9 years ago. He's right, and this is another way in which stories exist–those that have ended sometimes have sequels. It's a principle of magic that certain things have correspondences in other things, that certain patterns from the past affect the patterns of the future, that certain events in the future redeem certain events in the past.

And so it is, then.

Some stories end, some stories wait to be finished, some stories wait merely for more chapters. I'm going to several places that I've been before, places where a certain sense began to speak to me deeply. Many of my dreams have returned to this place, and sometimes I wonder if I haven't been spending most of the last decade attempting to understand what the hell that strange beckoning meant, why everything felt so odd yet so familiar, why I remember specific places there more vividly then I can remember what I had for dinner the night before.

Arrival

7 September (Rennes, France)

I arrived in Paris around 1pm, groggy. Since customs had been done in Iceland, arriving in Charles de Gaul was not difficult, except for the 50 pound bag on my back.

The rucksack I have is rather great, actually. It's heavy by itself, and incredibly heavy with everything I've got packed into it, but once you wear it, it's nearly weightless. That is, of course, until you're on a bus which suddenly stops and you find you've got much more mass than you remember.

From Paris, I took a train to Rennes. The train station is within part of the terminal (something which cannot happen in the United States, as everyone wants to blow us up and trains are socialist, right?). Not difficult to reach, not difficult to negotiate, but all liquids for sale cost roughly 3 American dollars. A pain au chocolat is still the correct price, as France has a long history of bread riots, so price gougers know better.

Arrived in Rennes around 6pm. The first thing which hit me was the air. I cannot describe it, nor could I possibly take a photo of it, but I can maybe tell you how it made me feel: Alive.

Like I'd breathed it before, in some other world for years, decades, perhaps an entire lifetime.

Your Face Is A Forest

The campground I'm staying in is quite good. It's nothing like an American camping ground: France has public, city-run campgrounds in almost every decent-sized city, and they're both plain and perfectly useful. This one happens to be in a wooded park, near several ponds...one could almost spend one's entire time within the park and the campground and feel one has fully vacationed, except, of course, for there being a city nearby.

And the city's quite excellent. After setting up my tent, I all but ran back to it (jet-lag is for losers), except on a bus. There's a bus directly from the campground to the centre-ville, and it takes about 20 minutes or so to get there.

I wandered for a few hours, purposefully without a map, turning corners into sudden explosions of ancient architecture (though most of what's here is no older than the 1600's) and streets thronged with people.

I got some street food (I'm sort of embarassed by its name, but it was good), took it to a square where punks were playing with their dogs and fashionably drest students were playing a Breton version of horse-shoes and ate, suddenly aware of something I hadn't quite experienced in a long time:

Relief.

I was here, in a place which has called (back) to me for years, and had nothing to do but live.

When I returned to the campground, I hung out with an Irish couple who drank me a bit too much and regaled me with stories of their homeland (Newgrange—I must go), their occasional ice-cream shop (Guinness ice-cream, it seems), their hopes to move to France. Maybe the most absurdly hospitable people I've met in quite some time--I had significant difficulty attempting to persuade them that I really didn't need to smoke all of their cigarettes and drink all of their wine. Also, I couldn't find camping fuel the first night, and the next day was a Sunday, so they let me borrow their cooking stove to make tea in the morning.

8 September

I slept maybe the first very deep, very restful slumber in months. Woke cold, the stars still out, rabbits everywhere. Felt damn good.

I saw Ian and Emily off (the aforementioned Irish folk) with some tea that I'd brought with me from Seattle, as the French tend towards weak tea. Even as I write this, a day later, I've still got Ian's Irish accent in my head, a funny thing to have remain but also quite welcome.

Spent maybe four hours in Rennes after this, exploring more, eating more pain au chocolat (this will be a recurring theme), and sitting in random places with fountains and wells of strange and wondrous design.

Wanderings

In a well in a square was a stone head, laying flat upon the water, looking in. Decapitated, it would seem, yet serene. I'm actually quite proud I got the reflection of the face, as I'm not generally a very good photographer. And I've got all sorts of other photos already, but only a few will have to suffice for now, as the computers in this internet cafe are hit or miss (some shut down immediately when I plug in a camera, some work perfectly well) and I'm currently on one towards the side of "miss." I like not having constant access to a computer. I like that I don't see many smartphones around here. I like that people are talking to each other–*everywhere*.

I dislike that I have to travel to another country to see this again.

No bitterness, though. Seattle's rather far away at the moment. I did a quick check on Facebook and confirmed that, yes, everyone is still posting pictures of what they had for dinner and yes, complaining about waiting a couple of minutes for a bus and yes, narrating their lives through tiny witticisms that sometimes land utterly flat.

I've been thinking about this a lot, particularly. Narrating one's life is quite crucial and I think probably universal. However, I've noticed there's plenty of times that I experience something and immediately wonder how to describe it to someone else. This–this is probably not good. Not everything is meaningful, not everything can be re-inscribed into the world of others (who really cares what you had for dinner?) or should be thus re-inscribed.

But obviously, some things can be and should be. Why tell story in the first place? Why write any of this at all, or read what others say?

Maybe we've gotten lazy, or maybe more desperate for material. Maybe going to France was a very, very good idea for me.

Nah. It was fucking brilliant.

As far as druid stuff goes, there's been plenty already. I found myself collecting crystalline cedar resin and had a woman stop and ask me, fascinated, what I was doing. Had my necklace shatter dramatically in front of a statue of a saint in a church (still not sure what that was about), and, last night, saw a toad hopping across my path and said hello to him. Not sure if it's quite common for toads to stop when you greet them instead of fleeing, or if it's quite common for them to let you pick them up after this. At the very least, he seemed a very, very nice toad.

Upon The Chemins

9 September

I had what should have been a bad day, except, well, no.

I wandered around the grande ville again for several hours and found myself getting oddly lost, like I was walking in a labyrinth. Mostly, I'd been trying to find that pool again, with the severed head. I wanted to think and read tarot and journal at it, because it felt oddly sacred…but no. No luck.

I walked for hours, getting progressively more lost, finding myself each time turning back upon the same alleys. But here's an interesting thing about labyrinths: they are mazes on the outside which walk you through similar, strange twists internally. Anyone who's walked a labyrinth as part of a ritual understands this, I imagine.

Where my mind was going, I'm not quite sure. I was everywhere and nowhere, stumbling repeatedly upon the same cathedrals, the same chapels.

Later, I went to ameliorate what was the most pressing problem of mine: lack of cooking fuel. The campsite shop had none, and I'd heard of a strange shopping center, about a mile and a half away from the campground, that would sell it.

Wanderings

From the center of the city I took a bus, listening to the conversations around me while still turning within my head. And I arrived, and oh gods....

Malls in the US terrify me. I've been to one in the space of maybe 6 years because of this, and that was with a fellow druid, and we were only there to get a sandwich. But I was now in another, except in France, and oh–

Culture shock comes for me when I go shopping for groceries. Upon return from Europe each time, I break down when I enter an American grocery store. And at some point it happens in Europe, too, surrounded by configurations which make no sense.

Still, found what I thought I was looking for, left, and cut across some back alleys and a chemin ('trail' in French, in Bretagne the word usually refers to the Old Tracks). There, I gorged on elderberries and blackberries and strolled with less care than before back to the campground.

But–oi. Gas canisters used to be standardized in Europe. The same one from the same company fit in everything they made, but it seems, unfortunately, they've caught on to the ridiculous absurd shit America does, where you always improve and therefore always make older stuff obsolete. That is, so you keep buying. I had to go back to the mall, this time to get a different cooking stove (the new and improved one which fits the three canisters I'd bought). Normally such a journey to undo something that didn't go correctly the first time really pisses me off, but at least I got to walk by more berries. I picked up a bottle of Breton cidre while I was at it, gathered more berries and flowers, and returned to my site, finally getting to make myself tea, and then dinner, and then a mulled cidre with the berries I'd gathered.

I'm not fully certain what happened next, and some of it is not for this conversation, but I found myself out in the woods, not exactly drunk but most definitely intoxicated by something intensely different from what I normally experience.

10 September

There was a transit strike, so I spent most of the day at my tent, reading, thinking, and organizing. Also, drinking more tea than one really ought (it'd been days, you know).

Most of the day I was in my head, dreaming, attempting to make sense of the world around me. No–this isn't quite true. Actually, I've been attempting to make sense of the world I left behind, now that there's a con-

Your Face Is A Forest

tinent and an ocean between myself and it.

Returned to the city, bought my train tickets for the next leg. In about an hour I leave for Carnac/Plouharnel, where I've been before. This is the place I've dreamt the most about, and the dream which compelled me to return to Bretagne took place there. It's littered with standing stones and wells and old tracks and chapels, and though I'll be there a few more days than I was here, I'm not sure it's going to be enough time.

I finally found that fountain with the severed head again. I'd circled it repeatedly the day before. This doesn't surprise me.

I may not be able to update for a few days, as the closest internet will be a 45 minute walk away, and I've much to do there.

Many of you are in my thoughts, by the way. I miss knowing there are people close by to talk to who know me.

11 September

I have almost no time at the moment, but I wanted to write something to you.

I left Rennes and got to Plouharnel/Carnac a few hours later and pretty much lost myself immediately. I almost didn't wait to set up my tent–I practically found myself running out onto the chemins, visiting as many holy sites as I could in a very short time before the sun set. I almost missed the closing of the only grocery store in Plouharnel on account of this fanaticism.

It's really damn hard to explain how insane this place is.

I arrived near 4pm, set up my tent, 'bavarded' a bit with the owners of the camping site (who haven't changed much since I saw them 9 years ago, though they've got two young children now). On my way to the site I got a bit lost, on account of getting off at the wrong stop, and ran into a group of old Breton women who preceded to flirt with me uncomfortably. One asked if I'd hitchhiked, and when I told her no but mentioned I'd considered it, she answered "someone as nice and attractive as you? People will stop."

As I said, after setting up the tent, I went for a long walk, visiting the chapel of Ste. Barbe (one of the oldest here) and several fountains which I'd remembered before. Walked until it was dark, headed back, made dinner and passed out to strange, scattered dreams.

Wanderings

12 September

I woke awfully early, took a shower, made breakfast (coffee, gallettes, jam) and decided to go for a short walk.

If, by short, one means 12 hours and 18 or so miles.

The path I chose was a series of linked chemins which go along the bay towards Carnac in the south. It meanders through gorse, heather, blackberries, and wind-contorted pines and firs, past and through old villages, oyster farms, fountains, lavoirs (baths, though they're a bit mucky and I have not used them) and insanely breath-taking views of the sea.

When I started out, the bay was near dry, gulls and herons feasting off of the crustaceans exposed to the air. There were huge piles of shells here and there, where the birds gathered their spoils and then left their refuse.

I forgot to bring food, or hadn't cared to, so I ate as many blackberries and unripe blueberries as I could handle. This is a lot, you should know, and my hands were stained purple by the time I reached Carnac-ville.

What can I say about this walk? I would show you things, photos, but–fuck.

I lost my camera.

When I arrived in Carnac, I headed first to the chapel of St. Cornaille (I think that's his name), one of the 6 founding saints of Bretagne (that is, on of the 6 Christian founders). I need to maybe stop going to greet saints, for as I fumbled for my camera which I'd been using extensively during the walk, I found it gone.

This was utterly frustrating. After walking around a bit, buying a pain-au-chocolat (of course) and a baguette, I started the walk home, retracing my steps to find where I must have lost the camera.

Thing is, it was getting quite dark. I could already feel the day fading, and I had not brought my flashlight. But I found myself obsessing over this camera and where I could possibly have lost it. I needed it, you see.

Well, sort of. This made me think about several things (walking for miles is great for thinking), including why I'd been taking so many photos in the first place. It was, mostly, for you, dear reader, dear friends. I don't resonate heavily with photos myself, unless they are extremely good, but I thought for certain this would be the best way to explain to you how fucking beautiful this place is, how strange and wondrous it is to come out from a copse of pine or oak to a small medieval village and then see the sea.

I walked extra, retracing my steps several times in order to find where I'd lost the fucking thing. It was getting quite close to sunset, I knew this was a lost hope, but I took another detour to check one last time.

Your Face Is A Forest

Nope.

I wonder, though. Did some higher part of myself leave it on the rocks on purpose? Or did I leave it at the chapel? Its loss has actually been a very good thing for me. Here's why: I'd see something profound, beautiful, breathtaking, Otherworldly, and immediately fumble for my camera, snap a couple of photos, check to see if I'd caught the image right, and then put it away and walk on.

That is, I stopped seeing things, except to see them for others. I realised this just as the sun was setting, just as I knew I had no hope of getting back before dark. I sat on a rock, frustrated, tired (my feet are mangled, by the way), and found myself seeing something unimaginable in its beauty.

The sun set over the bay, brilliant and dark hues of purples, violets, blues mixing with crimson reflecting off the water of the bay (the tide had come in fully now). Greens of seaweed floated like islands upon the water, and silver danced in the waves where the last whites of the sun hit. The stones of the shore are black, but also dun, as was the sand, though giving off a yellow-gold that seemed like trapped sunlight from the warm day.

I cried, but not from sadness.

13 September

Nothing happened today.

This is not true, of course. But most of it was in my head. I wrote a letter, I read Tarot and Ogham and a book (a fucking great one, by the way, called The Art of Pilgrimage). And I ate.

Mostly, I hobbled. I rather messed up my feet with that walk. They're better today, and I'm in the middle of another 10 mile walk.

Oh. One thing happened, I guess. After dark, I went for a walk and sat at a crossroads for several hours (probably 3 or 4, I'm guessing). Lit a fire. Stared at the sea and the stone carved with a triskelion. Called to something or someone. I suggest it. I'll have more to say on this later.

And I woke the next morning (but I'm not talking about this yet) to a dream of a giant sorting through my head.

Heather, Alder, Gorse

14 September

The days are stringing together like a tapestry I didn't know the soul could weave. The fourteenth? Where...that was the day with the alignments and the Deer and the Heather, the day I lost the camera? No, that was a different–that is the same.

All is always now, except not, because the sun sets and I get sleepy, and the sun rises and I awaken, and between those moments is every color in which life is painted, every note in which life is sung, every word in which the world breathes intself into our souls.

What happened? The 14th...that was samedi...yes, the deer.

I awoke, the dream of the giant sorting through my thoughts, my desire, his voice deep, his voice quaking, like an old lover I'd forgotten I had, who returned to ask who it was had visited my heart since he last went hunting. He held a fragment of cloth, a fragment of thought and asked, "whose was this?" And I had to answer that I hadn't met him yet, but intend to, and I awoke.

Breakfast is always a baguette, except that it was a baguette and eggs and tea and coffee and framboise-jam. I had awakened into ombre, shadow, feeling–was this the day of light? Of the fire? I think so.

Your Face Is A Forest

I sent off a letter (is it for this he was asking?) and went for a walk. There are abbeys, but not ancient. They are massive, dominating in their walled cloistered prayers, but they are only as old as Seattle, so they held less interest than other places. I like all ages of lovers, but not in architecture. They must be old enough to have great-grandfathered my great-grandmother for me to consider them worthy of my affection.

Still. I had a walking stick, finally. Pine, until later, when it became Alder. There is a pine grove across from the entrance to the Abbey of St. Michel. This does not surprise me, nor did the oak grove across from the alignments of Menec, but I'm not there yet.

A back path, a faded chemin. Heather in my pocket, because it was beautiful and I knew I would need to give it as a gift. When given the choice between stealing across private property and cutting through gorse, take the choice I didn't take. Gorse is friendly in that "hey I'm a little too drunk for this" sort of way. Gorse reminds me of the only time I was in San Francisco, at a bar with my then-lover whose finger was in a rather intimate place until I realised both of his hands were otherwise occupied. That stranger's finger?

That's Gorse. And it's beautiful, but overly friendly.

The chemins end, or continue onto roads before weaving back out of the interruption of modern transit. Walking on a paved part of a chemin is like walking through mud, yet less earthy, and louder. And there, at the side of the modern, I saw the corpse of a newly-dead fawn, its eyes open to the sky, unmourned perhaps. I found the use of the heather and bid it safe passage.

The Alignments: look. I can't tell you about them. I can't show them to you because of the camera. All I can say--they are old not in that ancient way but in that chthonic way, older than primeval, radiating an intensity that isn't for us any longer, or not yet, not until we've learned the intensity that is for us. But you should see them anyway, and stand in the oak grove across from them and be very, very quiet.

I watched a wedding begin at the chapel of St. Corentin. I felt I needed to. I did.

And then another long walk home, to dinner, to stars, and to a nearby...rave. I slept through it. It was for the wedding guests. A bunch of them were crying afterwards. Raves, I guess, could do this.

Wanderings

15 September

Another day of rest. Little to say until evening, when I walked one last time to the chapel of Ste. Barbe. I don't know why it draws me more than the others...perhaps because she's the only saint who hasn't taken something from me, yet. Long story.

I had a dream months ago. I was in a house, and I was leaving, and I tried to go up a path (a chemin, it would turn out), and two men blocked me. The first was in shadow, the second in light, but "his a face still forming" (--Eliot), and they would not let me leave. The one in shadow smiled, like he was waiting for me, and the one in light said, only, "did you forget your recorder? You should not forget your recorder."

I brought my recorder to the chapel just before sunset and played. At first I was alone, and then later others entered, sitting, listening. I stopped at some point, afraid I was disturbing the silence, until a man with a young daughter said, "C'est mieux avec la musique," and so I continued.

The song I played was not one I'd heard before. I don't feel like I made it up, more that it seemed an old song still echoing off the stones, one that I picked up. It's hard to explain, but certain notes sounded better within those old walls, and certain progressions of these notes were better than others, and next thing you know you have a song, and it seems best described as the song of that place. And as she was leaving, an old woman bowed her thanks to me.

And then a final visit to wells, and a farewell to the place. I tied a bit of blue scarf to two elder trees growing in the water of a fountain, joining them together, and their combined branches made a gate that I looked through and found to be the same place I'd sat a few nights ago, the crossroads, three chemins meeting.

16 September

I left in the morning. My Alder staff in hand, rucksack on my back, treading one last time down the alleys and streets to the place where a bus would take me to a train to Quimper.

Someone stopped. She smiled, waved, and gave me a thumbs-up.

A little while later, a car honked, and both of the passengers waved and said, "merci."

Were they thanking me for visiting? For playing in the chapel? There were so many people in there that one or two of them could have been those people. They all looked familiar. They can't have seen all the trash I

Your Face Is A Forest

picked up around the standing stones (look, kids–if you're gonna fuck in the telluric springs, fucking bring your condom wrappers with you on the way out, yeah?).

Or maybe they do this to everyone. Still, it felt–warm. Happy. Right.

The train to Quimper did not take long. I was starting to feel a bit feverish, and it's likely that I've gotten a bit ill. Laying on the ground all the time, often when it's raining, is probably not incredibly good for the constitution in the short term. Long term? Probably fucking fantastic.

Quimper is…fucking dark. Alder everywhere, and beautiful people, and a sense of lust and madness and poverty. I want to live here. Dominated by the Cathedral of St. Corentin (him again…), founding mythically by King Gradlon after the sinking of the city of Ys (long story, and I hope to tell it better someday soon), the confluence of three rivers, hills dividing the city, flanking the valleys in which people live.

Yet again, I tore away from my camp site just after setting up the tent and walked, walked…

I gotta stop doing this. I ended up on one of the hills, which is where I was headed, because I didn't want to go to the Cathedral of Corentin yet. And I'm on this massive hill which is hard to reach and fenced off, and there's a woman, drest well, behind a fence in a mental-hospital. The hill is covered by psychiatric and other specialty hospitals.

She said, "bonne nuit," and I couldn't answer, and not because I didn't understand.

At The Crossing Of Three Rivers

17 September

I slept really hard that night. The rains began, as Quimper seemed always misted, greyed, and doused of much life. But, well, no–anyone who's lived in Seattle knows full well that a city can be grey and rainy yet still pulsing with some inner life–it's just a question, then, for anyone to consider what sort of life courses through its streets.

Quimper's fucking gorgeous, and fucking dark. It's Kemper in Breton, or "confluence," as it sits upon three rivers which meet before flowing out to the sea. These rivers cut gouges through the forested hills of the capitol of Finistere ("Penn ar Bed" in Breton, or "end of the world…" and it feels like it.), meet, flow away, sluggishly, as the people quickly walk by it along the quays.

I don't mean to make it sound depressing–it kind of is, actually, but–but I want it. I want to live there, almost desperately, and this urge surprises me. It urged me on continuously, treading across the cobbles through the medieval warrens each of which seems, ultimately, to lead to the Cathedral of Saint Corentin.

Your Face Is A Forest

I finally visited the place, as no matter which direction I walked from it, I'd be there again. Saint Corentin is one of the 7 founding saints of Christian Brittany, attributed not just to the usual sets of miracles but also of living on an ancient, lost island city similar to Atlantis and multiplying fish just like Jesus.

If you go there, don't use the holy water. It's been pissed in, and not by me. Possibly the angry drunk punks outside, possibly by some angry Breton. And there's lots, and I don't know how to explain it, but I think something's waking up there. Not in the Cathedral, nor underneath, but something behind the dazed look on some of the faces of the Bretons you see on the street.

I don't want to tell you about the Cathedral of Saint Corentin or about Saint Corentin himself. I'd rather tell you what I heard someone explain to me in a bar: "He took away our joy. He made us safe, him and the other Christians, but we lost our joy." This from an atheist.

There are pages and pages I could write about the modern Breton culture, Breton nationalism (which looks less like nationalism and more like cultural survivalism, from what I've seen), and the conversations I had. But I'm paying by the minute here at an internet cafe, and I'd like to study it more. But it's fascinating to see people actively attempting to regain their past and weave it into their present, even at a time of economic misery (Quimper, like much of Bretagne, is going through a hard recession).

There's more I'd say on this, but I need to go back to understand.

18 September

Another hard rain and a strange darkness, woken into after strange dreams. The rivers speak, the hills speak, but I do not know their language, and I think they fear they've forgotten how to speak.

Woke into the rain, into the sharp edge of solitude.

"Ah–zu want zur Tea in my tente?"

I looked at her. Breton to the core, straight out of a Jean Jeunet film. Her tent next to mine–I'd seen her a few times, said bonjour and all of that (it's a secret, by the way–want someone to remember you? say hello to them. Otherwise you don't exist. It's like all of life) but had given little thought to her beyond this, wrapped so deeply in my own thoughts.

"Zur tente-not so..how do zu say, sec?"

"Oh, it's dry," I replied in French. This tent, it should be noted, has been excellent for the rains of Bretagne.

Wanderings

"Oh, good." She seemed downtrodden. I felt diminished at my refusal, as she appeared to be.

I got to thinking...why do I refuse the kindness of strangers? I mostly survived off of it when I was younger, and it's essential when traveling. What–what made me change?

I suspect Seattle. Like extricating oneself from brambles, or worse, extricating ivy from a forest, I don't think I can quickly explain the tendrilled fear-of-the-other that city taught me. But I'd been aware of it for quite some time, and remained so that day.

I roamed about the city for a while, thinking on this matter, thinking on the inexplicable dreams and the subtle, garbled whispers from the city. I wrote some, read some more, and got lost.

If you want to know a place in which you don't live, get lost. Forget your map, get rid of your GPS (I've multiple stories of running into tourists looking for places in Seattle which were directly in front of them, yet their phones told them to keep walking), and walk 'till your feet bleed.

I fucking fell in love with the darkness of the city that day, its dripping clouds soaking me, its back alleys and hidden alcoves becoming not shelter but gateways.

19 September

Sometime in the middle of the night I awoke to an animal noise. Snorting, rustling, very close to my ear. In that state between sleeping and waking, I say to myself, "Oh. It's a boar. She's hungry, poor thing," and then fall back to sleep.

I wake to find my tent covered in la merde d'oiseux and find the packaging for all of my food scattered about, and a package of salami oddly missing.

The woman next to me approached again. "A wild boar," she said in French. "They come from the hills."

I did my best to clean up the mess, and then, a little later, the woman approached again. I noticed I was going into "no" mode before even hearing her offer, so I checked myself and listened.

"My friend and I–we are going to an old medieval sea fort, perhaps you would come with us?"

I would have been an idiot to say no.

The deux Laurences (feminine name) have been friends since early school. One utterly Breton, the other utterly Gaulish, the both more fun

Your Face Is A Forest

than any two friends have right to be. They drove us all to Concarneau, a strange castle-on-the-sea much like a small St. Malo. For hours we wandered around the old ramparts, talking, eating Breton cookies, laughing at everything. Me and two middle-aged women and a medieval fort.

I learned more about Bretagne from those two than any of the books I've read, and more about how I am being perceived. Breton Laurence told me that she was certain, "you–you are not much like the other ones of your friends, right? I mean, you are strange, in a very good way. Also, an American in Quimper? How rare!"

She seems to be right. In fact, everywhere I've gone except in Rennes, with everyone I've spoken, it is the same refrain. Not many Americans visit Bretagne, and in many cases I was the first some of them had met.

It felt fucking wonderful to be around people, to have conversation with others, and, in addition, I'll admit that I wasn't aware that my French had become so good that I could spend the day with two people and speak nothing but.

Later: dinner, and then…a gay bar.

I needed to fortify myself for the next day, you see. Also…Breton men are excruciatingly gorgeous, and the idea of being a bit closer to them than merely passing on the street m'interesse'd greatly.

There's one in Quimper (there used to be three, but like many other places in the city, the others recently closed). Bar 100 Logique, I believe. I arrived around 9, sat myself at the bar next to the four other people there, and began to write in my journal.

5 beers, 2 shots, and three hours later I walked myself home. I bought one of those drinks, the others were all from the (very charming, rather gorgeous) bartender and the two old Breton gents with whom I spoke for the majority of the night. Apparently, "c'est mignon" (it's cute) how I speak French, fumblingly, a little bro-ish, and often overly formal. Also, I'm otherwise mignon, I was told.

Walking through ancient cobbled streets drunk is something not to be missed. It's become a habit of mine to walk thusly and shout "older than shit!" at cathedrals (a habit I picked up in Strasbourg), but I was a bit more subdued. I'd forgotten mostly what I meant to do the next day, though a few of the people at the bar to whom I'd mentioned it suggested I was quite "fou" (foolish), and wished me "bon courage."

A car pulls up next to me. "Oi–Reeed. It's Rafael."

It was the bartender.

Wanderings

"I will drive you home," he said.

Another offer from a stranger, and I assented, as I'm not sure I would otherwise quite have made it. He dropped me off at the entrance of the camping place, bid me farewell, and I passed out.

20 September (Menez Hôm)

Rafael had, at some point in the night or earlier the next morning, left an envelope on my tent containing a note with his phone number and a request that, if I ever return to Quimper, I call him. I certainly shall.

A bit more hung over than perhaps I should have been, I gathered my stuff and took a bus 30 miles to the north to Menez Hôm, an ancient hill in the "black mountains" of Finistere known to have been a religious site for druids. They'd found statues of Brighid in martial dress and old walls with no apparent evident purpose.

The place is more storied than any other place I've visited. And I don't know how to tell you about my story there. It might not matter. I need to go back. I saw, along one of the trails, an identical landscape to a vision I'd seen a few months ago, and in the spot where I'd seen a tower in the vision I saw instead–well.

I don't know. I'll be going back. I'll need to return to find out why there are recently carved Norse runes in the pavement in places, and what at least one of the six dreams I had as I slept under a full moon amongst corn without a tent meant.

But anyone who knows the old Bardic myths knows that one does not hide from certain goddesses amongst corn.

21 September

Nothing happened this day, except walking back down the hill in a confused daze, returning to Quimper, packing for Rennes, and indulging in a pizza (French pizza is strange) and sleeping and having more dreams.

Suffice it to say, however, this–I shall miss the fuck out of Quimper–
–and I shall return.

Penn Ar Breizh

I've been asking myself many questions to which I do not care to know the answer. Rhetorical games with myself, I guess. Unnecessary, perhaps, but useful. And in writing this, I should admit that I talk to myself–a lot. Sometimes I answer back, yes, and sometimes I argue with myself. Mostly I just chuckle a bit, particularly now, particularly often.

After the night on Menez Hôm, a resounding inquiry voiced itself: "What are you going to do now, without your fear?"

This is deeper than it appears. A long time ago, someone who cared for me deeply stated that my politics and way of life were extinguishable from my coping mechanisms, and he was, at that time, utterly correct.

On the surface, there are two clear ways of confronting fear: the first, going directly at, towards, and through that which creates anxiety. The typical opposite, in most estimations, is merely running away from it.

But, no. There's a third way. Build yourself a magnificent castle, or a city ringed by fortresses in which you foster life inside. Invite your friends, artists, musicians, poets, priests, artisans–create a world within a wall, and enlarge those walls when needed, and never once mention to yourself the founding terror of the place. People will come from miles to visit what's been built, what it inspires in them, but, of course, the unacknowledged core of its existence remains unspoken.

Wanderings

The experience on that mountain, asleep under the full moon without a tent, the dreams and visions and whispers ripped me from my fear, and, to be honest, I sort of miss my fear in the way that one might miss an abusive lover or a gilded cage.

I'm not explaining this well. I often don't. My words rarely mean what I intend them to mean, and I haven't even quite come to grips with precisely what it is I'm even trying to say. But something is missing, and it's weird to find it gone.

22 September (Alban Elued/Equinox)

I left Quimper with a strange heaviness. Really–those more minded in the earth and the material will certainly find my explanation problematic or just silly, but it felt like every step towards the train station became more difficult, like the city was…pouting. Or maybe I was. I don't know, but I made certain promises to myself and certain promises, aloud, to the rivers of that city that I shall either return or help build a world in which others come to see its beauty, come to hear the whispering of the water flowing through it like veins, come to stand in awe of the ancient, waiting spirit of the hills. Mayhaps, even, come to learn and unravel (better than I'll ever be able to) its mysteries.

I'm still haunted by the woman I mentioned, behind a fence at a mental hospital. She seemed–happy, but wild. I've worked for years with the mentally-ill, but there's something fiercely different in her. And she, on a hill, seemed maybe to have heard the same thing I did. This is terrifying.

This is also comforting.

After these promises, my pack felt lighter, my steps more certain, and I made it to the station with plenty of time to sit and smoke. As a side note, and as a matter of responsibility, I should mention it's often unwise to travel on Sundays in France, as there are either few–or, in the case of Quimper, no–buses. Such a thing is quite inconvenient if one is travelling, but seeing almost an entire city thronging the streets on the same day each week is not all bad, I guess.

I talked at length with a Senegalese man, rolled him cigarettes (have I mention I failed at quitting?) and took the train to Rennes.

Waiting for a bus in Rennes, I got caught in the middle of a game of street soccer: happily inebriated youths laughing and only half-apologizing when the ball hit an old woman in the head. I felt lumbering (70 pounds heavier with my three bags, yeah?) and overheated and a little grumpy until one of them circled me a few times, clownishly, and then stepped on each of my boots with his bare-feet and pretended I was a statue of a giant, too-solemn and too-somber.

It's hard to take yourself seriously after this. The bus came, I got on with almost a hundred other people, and an old woman offered me her seat as I apparently looked more needy than her. I accepted, and then found the few people who'd surrounded me in their game thronging me now, laughing and pulling out instruments. They started playing, and then others on the bus started humming along, and again, that dream from before, "did you forget your recorder? You should not forget your recorder" returned and suddenly I'm playing along with them, an old Breton song called Tri Martolod.

Followed them to a park (all my stuff with me, still), played some more music, drank, and then, hours later, finally set up my tent and, inadvertently, passed out.

23 September

I spent the morning preparing my stuff to leave Bretagne altogether. The next day, I was to go to Strasbourg (from whence I'm writing this), so I wandered one last time around Rennes, my eyes lingering upon every tree in my vision, the Breton streets I won't see again for awhile, and the people.

I wish I could better explain Bretons. Actually, look–I wish I could better explain Bretagne. I was only there for less than three weeks, and I feel like it's soaked itself into my skin, into my lungs, into my soul.

I worry a bit, though, that the more I attempt to explain it, the more distant it becomes now, sitting here in an apartment in an Alsatian city, far away from the rivers and the stones and alder. Also, the magpies, the toads, and the (unseen) boar. The streets, the fairy-tale quality of the clouds, the setting sun torching the sky in brilliant colors. The feel of the rain--even the inconvenient rain.

In a daze, or perhaps in a dream I wandered those streets one last time, eating another pain au chocolat and an apple turnover (chausette au pomme, or apple-sock). I stumbled into a Breton book store and found a copy of an academic text concerning the legend of the Isle of Ys, and then returned to my tent, made myself dinner, and wandered one last time into the woods, sitting alone as the sun set, candles lit about me, watching the stars peer through the clouds, listening one last time to the trees and the birds and whispering my own farewell. Not adieu, but more au plus-tard, not "good-bye" but "until a bit later."

Wanderings

Another question I've asked myself is this: at what point does a pilgrimage end? I left the place where I've lived for 13 years, and since I won't be returning there anytime soon, the answer "when you return" doesn't suffice.

Bretagne pretty much screams fairy-tale, bleeds ancient gods, rains lost knowledge. And I left Bretagne, and though I did not wish for my pilgrimage to end, I thought perhaps it must have. Alsace is not Bretagne, no ancient druidic sites or dark forests, yeah?

Ha.

Walled Cities & Blind Saints

24 September: (Rennes/Paris/Strasbourg)

I'm not sure if I mentioned, but the campsite where I stayed, run by the city of Rennes (almost every French city has one, and they've all been rather damn good), is utterly over-run by rabbits. Hundreds. Step out of your tent and there they are, glaring back at you as if to ask what you're looking at.

I'm looking at hordes of rabbits, that's what.

It took little time to leave Rennes in the morning. In fact, I'd gotten so good at packing up my stuff by the end of my Bretagne journey it seemed almost a shame not to need to do so before sunrise, with the stars still out and the moon just setting, again.

In France, all *grandes lignes* (major train-lines) pass through Paris. It isn't that Paris is central to France, but mostly because Paris considers itself to be. And as much as I adore the city, I've utterly dreaded it equally. Imagine the most graceful people you've ever met, wearing clothes which fit precisely perfectly and are always precisely the exact weight and coverage required for whatever the weather.

Now, imagine they built a city that extends near infinitely in all directions, with a transit system with precisely the amount of space required for said

Wanderings

graceful people, tunnels through which they seem to glide effortlessly (yet expending enough energy to remain sleek). Meals which are precisely the perfect size for their bodies and incomes (which are gracefully significant), doors dimensioned according to their needs, and toilets so discrete they don't need to sit, only bend their slender but well-formed legs slightly, nor use paper to clean themselves afterwards because, well, Parisiens are perfect.

I dread Paris for all these reasons and more (including the fact that respiration seems to require money, the city is so expensive), and I had forgotten that, in order to change from a train coming from the west of France to a train going to the east, you have to go to a different station. As a matter of fact, I realized this pretty much 10 minutes before arriving in Paris, and found myself, my graceless, *maladroit* self navigating the Paris metro between Gare Montparnasse and Gare d'Est.

The French metro has these bizarre pneumatic turnstiles, precisely timed and sized for a Parisien to pass through. Fail and you are trapped, embarassingly, with all your bags toppled upon you as strange tubes attempted to close around you and the sleek and near invisible Parisiens suddenly become quite visibly present, as they're trapping you against the turnstyle which won't open for you any longer and oh! you forgot to take your ticket back out of the machine.

Actually, that was last time. Maybe one of the greatest accomplishments of my adult life occured this day. I wasn't trapped. I found my way immediately through the Metro. Only one Parisien dog barked at me. I even exchanged kinds and humorous words with some Parisiens, who laughed at what I said. I was all grace, all sleekness, all…Paris.

For, like, 15 minutes. Then I spilled some coffee when I got on the train for Strasbourg.

In Strasbourg, I was met by my friend Duf at the station. We met 9 years ago, through a punk friend of hers who grabbed my then-lover and I along on a drinking binge our fourth day in Strasbourg, eventually inviting us to the house of his friend (who unknown to me until a few days ago, had explicitly asked him no longer to bring home strays just before he brings us home) to await her return.

When she got hom,e she's, like, pissed. Dead silent. Our French sucks, he's unhelpful, and she's eating with an aura of contemplative rage. And I'm a bit drunk. And when she's finished eating, she asks, "who the fuck are you?"

Such events, you should know, are precisely how to make good friends.

Your Face Is A Forest

25 September: Inside

You would think it would be an utter relief to be inside of an apartment after so much camping. And it is, actually, but there's a bit of adjustment required. Sleeping under stars and trees, rising and sleeping when you awaken and when you pass out, and, you know, pissing wherever's convenient: all rather liberating habits. Not so good for being in-of-doors, and it took me a while to re-civilize. I felt a bit like a savage wild wood-man, unsure what to do with himself.

But society's got its benefits. Clean clothes, showers, not needing to haul water, and, fuck, the food's been damn nice. The night before, we ate a Raclette, a bit like a reverse fondue, or think a chinese hot-pot except with meat and cheese–one melts ones own cheese over a burner, scrapes it over potatoes, and eats. Simple yet utterly profound. We ate this with Duf's two neighbors, and one of them was assigned to babysit me today. Where do you take a man uncertain what to do with himself in a city after the forest?

To watch monkeys, of course. He and I spent most of the day watching animals, playing music (I've got like 8 new songs I want to learn, mostly Yiddish) and hanging with Czech punks in a city square. The city is like a forest, without trees, a world full of animals who talk in a language that isn't quite mine yet, but a little easier than Willow or Birch.

26 September: The Animals I've Seen

I'm not quite in order here, as there's much more to tell than I've got the mind for at the moment. I feel I should tell you about Strasbourg and its history, or the epic sandstone cathedral, or the old mills and gorgeous canals, the Alsatian architecture and the insane food.

What I really want to talk about, however, is Keups, Duf's dog. Or, that is, animals in general. It's strange to say, but I think I can say it honestly–I never really noticed animals until this trip. I've given attention to certain birds who seem to try to tell me something, sure, or to my former cat, or to the occasional raccoon, but, really, never to this degree.

I woke this day remembering a dream I'd had in the night: I was surrounded by animals who spoke a language I understood, that I'd had to learn, and they told me something both relieving and obscure: "we're glad you'll take our side." A friend mentioned an animal spirit had prompted him to write me. Another who works with that same spirit praised my writing. And I'd sensed that same spirit at my back (I'm not much for animal guides, or wasn't until…now, I guess).

Wanderings

I've held a toad for the first time in my life walking down a chemin. A boar ate my salami (which, someone recently pointed out, is a bit cannibalistic). Ravens have stared me down, as have rabbits (and I'm not sure which is more fierce). I watched a mole play by a holy well. I've finally seen magpies, and a large hawk relatively close. And, well, there's Keups, the dog, who's more fun than you can imagine. Strange, though, to realize I've never given attention to what the animals are really on about until now.

Certainly studying Druidry has given me a prompting for this, but for the most part I've just been out (sometimes literally) hugging trees. But I've been out-of-doors for several weeks with no internet, no phone, and no companion, in a foreign country. This, certainly, has helped too.

Oh, and Keups is damn cool. There's a running joke now that we're in love and going to get married.

27 September: Thoughts on the City

Strasbourg is a walled city, walled also by fortresses. Strategic, and all that. Massive cathedral on an island made by canals (really, I could show you photos, but why bother? Come see it yourself, please.) Full of people, absurdly full of life. Gorgeous, enticing. Precisely the sort of place in which one wants to lose oneself. Good friends already, fascinating sights, more than enough to permanently distract.

Cities are like this, and European cities much more. For a gay man, a city's pretty much essential to survival, but for a druid or any other spiritually-incline person, it presents a massive problem. Not so much forest, not so much nature, and almost no quiet.

I think most spiritual people face this, and it's recently become a more looming difficulty for me. When you start giving attention to intimations and intuitions and spirits and such, downtown's an almost painful place to be. All the reasons why cities are alluring to those seeking culture and freedom become distractions and barriers to spiritual pursuits. The choices are typically: lose oneself in the everyday and its demands and sacrifice the voice of the soul, or cloister oneself away from everything in order to listen to the soul but sacrifice the ability to manifest any truths thus gleaned into the world.

Balance is near impossible. Coming out of the intense silences and whispers of Bretagne to the life and press of Strasbourg has been a bit difficult. To be honest, I hadn't even noticed what was happening to me, until my host stated that it seemed like I needed time alone.

Your Face Is A Forest

Oh, right.
After six hours to myself, thinking, writing by a river, reading, watching the world from an attention less direct, I felt eminently better. Returned, drank with Duf and her neighbors and another who'd I'd met with her 9 years before, more alive, less torn between the now and the eternal.

28 September: The Blind Saint, The Sorceress, & The Pagan's Wall

So, huh. Again, wasn't sure if I was still on pilgrimage until today.

For not having seen me for 9 years, my friend certainly divined the utterly perfect place to take a whimsical, melancholy student of Druidry just out of several weeks in Bretagne, having a bit of trouble adjusting to society again.

We left near 9 in the morning with her friend Guillame, driving a bit north of Strasbourg to an Alsatian mountain named for the patron saint of blindness, Sainte Odile. Story's rather simple–sometime in the 7th century, a blind girl was baptised and found her sight returned to her. Her father kills her brother by beheading him, she brings him back to life, and then her father's okay with her becoming Christian instead of Pagan, like him. The story's a bit different from St. Barbara (only one of two saints I seem to get along with so far), who's father built a tower to keep her from marrying a Christian and then God struck him dead with lightning.

And, like all kinds of other Christian saints, she, of course, decides to build a monastery on the site of an ancient Pagan mountain, where there's a holy well. And, interestingly, parallel to the story of Saint Gwenole and Saint Corentin, she builds her holy place on the top of a mountain already ringed with strange, ancient fortifications.

That is, Mont Saint Odile is not very different from Menez-Hom, the visions at which still haunt me severely.

Ringing the mountain, towards the top, are strange fortifications with unknown purpose. Called Maennelstein in German and Le mur de Paien (The Pagan Wall) in French, it crowns the hill just under a site called Le grotte des druides (the Druid Grotto), the holy springs (there are several, one of which is said to cure blindness), and the summit where Sainte Odile built her monastery.

Guillaume chanced to mention the Dahu, a mythical beast like a goat except with two legs longer than the other two so it can ascend sideways.

Wanderings

There's another connection between Mont St. Odile and Menez Hôm: Dahut, the sorceress who drowned the city of Ys and who was said to have been drowned in turn by St. Corentin, is also said to have been turned into a Dahu, and if my memory serves me correctly, St. Odile in at least one place I've read is one of the saints said to have done this.

I need a library, like, now.

Also, not that I've been necessarily keeping score, but I've gotten to see two saint's relics now, the skull of a Franciscan saint in Quimper (said to bring fortune, of all things) and the sarcophagus of Saint Odile.

I leave Strasbourg on Monday for Berlin. I'm not yet certain what I'll find there. More than likely, just as now and before, more questions I never thought to ask.

Gates

There are gates everywhere. Doors, if you will. Cracks in walls which open when you push, gaps between things into which your thoughts can fit, squeeze through, and enter.

Some gates are made of light. Sunlight filtered through trees hitting stone. Sunlight filtered through trees refracted on water. Light dancing, still, not what it was, not what it will be when you look away. Starlight through pines. Candlelight against leaf.

Some of darkness and shadow. The abyss between Elder at night, the blackness of open cave, the un-seeing of closed eyes in sleep, the depths in the soul where the heart's light does not always reach.

Most are outside, but they are also in. Doors within are there but overgrown, hidden, like ruins of ancient forts and temples covered in vine and fallen tree. Cleared, the keys found, they can be entered, and they lead not to more inside, but an Other outside.

Death, too, is a door, but it is one we enter and choose to close behind us. And I have never felt so alive.

Wanderings

29 September

Mornings in my friend's apartment in Strasbourg were always the correct pace needed to come to consciousness, with gentle proddings from her ever-eager dog who'd become for me quite the companion.

It was a Sunday, a day sacred from commerce and most (but never all, a fact most forget and I really think they should not) work. And the last day of the bike I'd rented with Duf's help (the deposit was not steep, but on an American bank card the release of the funds takes another two weeks past the return).

Words should be said regarding the riding of bikes in medieval cities. That is, oh, fuck yes. Do it. Cobbles are as bumpy as you imagine they will be, and also a lot more fun than you'd think. Race and dart and dodge between cars attempting to navigate streets made for horses instead of wagons of steel, glance suddenly at looming antiquity jolting out between 400 year-old alleys, lock your bike next to the 700 or so others, and go drink a beer. Much is made of bike-culture in liberal cities like Seattle, but, really, events like Critical Mass are only solidarity rallies for people who haven't the fortune of living in Europe.

Duf and I rode to Germany. I'm a bit tempted to leave this statement stand for those of you with less geographical knowledge, but I try to be honest in these. It was only a few kilometers across the Rhin river (not Rhine, not Rhon, but Rhin). There's a park on either side of the border, a sort of unity memorial (that is, hey, let's not fight bloody wars again for awhile, see, maybe these trees will help? And of course I think that trees always help).

After returning the bike (with some sadness, I'll admit), I walked about the city again for another five hours. I find I sometimes cannot stop walking, even when tired. The feel of stone under foot, even through boots, is profound, welcome, comforting, like treading slightly-cool water on an excruciatingly hot day.

Connection to the ground below you, the slow, almost meditative speed by which one must walk long distances–it is profound, and I do not think you can know a place without walking through it.

Your Face Is A Forest

30 September - 1 October

Early in the morning I left Strasbourg for Offenburg, a small town in Germany at the foothills of the Schwarzwald. So, Ridigul (the aforementioned punk street-musician who'se name I'm sure I've misspelled) and I went to Offenburg to stay with his twin brother.

There's a term I came up with after my first trip to Europe: stupid tax. It describes the excessive prices one pays in any place because one is foreign or strange to it. Purchasing something that costs less just a few blocks further, buying the wrong transit pass (or the correct one but using it wrong), being ignorant of national holidays or Sunday closures and failing to plan accordingly, etc. You pay the first day no matter what, but the longer you stay in a place and the more observant you are, the less you must pay each day afterward.

A train from Strasbourg to Berlin costs 160 euro and takes 6 hours. I had been fretting not having purchased this ticket before, and as the deadline for buying it swiftly approached, I got a bit grumpy at the idea of spending so much (I can live for two weeks in most of the places I've been for this cost).

As it turned out, however, I did not need to. Ridigul informed me of a different means, also by trains but slower, taking 12 hours instead of 6 but costing 40 euro. Having lots of time, I decided this sounded rather welcome: 12 hours to think while staring at the German countryside is precisely the sort of thing I realise I find fun now.

Also something I find fun now is playing music with twin German street musician brothers in a small town for an entire day. Coffee, bratwurst, *neuwein* (new wine–like grapejuice, but alcoholic and cheap), accordion and guitar and two of the best voices I've heard in a long time. And then onion-cake (quiche, except with about 60 onions, and I know this because I chopped them all and still smell like them four days later) and maybe a bit too much beer and maybe a little too little sleep, and then, the next morning, 12 hours of train travel.

I'm not sure what to say about this trip, except that if one's just spent four weeks in France, the first three of which filled with the most profound spiritual experiences of ones life thus far, 12 hours in-between places is a great escape. In transition, between realms, un-rooted, shuttled between worlds–one is safe to contemplate ones life without interruption, without concern, without direct experience (except through the windows of a fast-moving train).

Wanderings

I started the journey near 9am, arrived in Berlin around 10pm and at the place of my friend Birga near 10.30, crashing out but not before taking in the strange, welcome, almost breathing air of this city.

I'm here now, writing from an internet cafe after having stared at my favorite canal for an hour in the sunlight (which inspired the words which begin this dispatch). I've not much else to say, as Berlin demands experience, makes detachment an act of suicide, makes mediation criminal. I'll find some stuff to say, certainly–I always do. But let this suffice for now, and, to repeat: I've never felt so alive.

You

I have drawn song from stone and air through wood in an ancient chapel so obscure none knows when it was built. I have listened by stones worn by time and fierce wind as the sun set, listening for the echoes of their meaning at their feet amongst gorse and heather. I have stood before the skull of an urchin made holy in a cathedral radiating authority and control over brooding spirits waiting for the return of their time.

Upon a worn mountain I waited, exhausted, as the visions and dreams poured through the moon's reflected light upon the shaking heads of corn, felt the rain upon my head as the chill set in, and stood, near-blinded, staring out into the landscape of which my dreams had been mere reflection.

By rivers I've whispered back to river-goddesses too-eager to have someone to hear them, hill-spirits deadened to their own voices by centuries of neglect and rape, and trees laughing without mirth at my attempts to speak their language.

Over ancient cobbles, through narrow alleys, by wells and fountains and worn statues I've trudged, unhurried like toad and turtle, burdened like ox, bound to earth, bound to what I carry.

And here is a city, old like ice and new like rain, curious like glaciers, breathing like mountains.

Wanderings

I don't know how to speak of Berlin. I will tell you what I have done, I will wield dulled words to carve symbols from what remains always unspoken. Had I better art, I'd speak only myth. Myth is truth wrapped in mystery where it survives time, survives the present and its concerns and weaknesses. It bridges past and future into an always-now which is no present but that which the present only shadows, only reaches for. It is the correspondence between life and love, or death and the eternal.

Berlin is myth. Like the gods, like ourselves.

2 October

Wake in the morning within a massive flat, once thrice its size 'till the inhabitants split its space for others. Crawl down carefully, backwards, the ladder to the 10-foot high loft only half-way reaching to the ceiling, wander out into the cavernous kitchen where the communal-renters share coffee and *fruehstuck* with you.

Speak to an old friend, met in another city neither of you liked. Listen to her happiness, the ferocity of life coursing through her words, the serene wonder of the world in her eyes and remember that this is not strange for this city.

Leave the building down echoing stairs into a courtyard, through a gate into another courtyard, through yet another into a world you almost forgot existed outside this home. People strolling, walking, rushing but unstressed towards bakeries, towards food stands, towards work that starts later than most societies would allow. Down steps into a tunnel breathing warmth and old metal dust towards the rushing of underground trains which feel so familiar you are sometimes surprised you've paid for the trip. Up other stairs into another city which is the same, by a canal lined with willows and sycamore and chestnut. Walk further in, farther over stone and bridge to where already people lunch at tables under awnings sprayed with graffiti like the stones beside them, a city inked in missives, tattooed and henna'd, the surface of the buildings like the soil of the earth in which our lives are lived, into which our deaths are composted into more and more and more life.

Can there be too much life? Not if there is death. Death is not the product of life, it is its mother, the fallen tree the widow's kind funerary rites, the spring the maiden's blossoming.. Death is our mother, filling the world with life, these streets with life, this air with–

Your Face Is A Forest

Drink. Walls covered in fake pink fur, the smokiest, coziest uterus you've ever re-visited. You know you will reek the next morning, you know the music's horrible, you know you shouldn't run your fingers through the wall-fur so grey you're not certain you don't see pink only because you know you're supposed to. You are in a womb which is a bar which is a sacred site to you, not an old druid circle or an ancient tomb, but holy nonetheless, and a bit nauseating, a bit gross, and you are glad of it.

3 October

Wake in the morning to coffee, not where you started the morning before. Walk from the place and find it noon, and others are waking, and it is a holiday, and the autumn air, cold, breathes out the stale smell of beer and smoke. Beyond it is another smell, a quality to air we've no words for. We've forgotten to name those things, but remember that, in another time of freedom before hatred marched through streets, they'd named it a song.

The song's ridiculous, but it makes you smile as you sing it in your head with more coffee in hand, powder from what an American president called himself in your beard. The air, the luft (*luft luft*), and you reel in wonder until you catch the light upon the canal and remember what you were trying to remember to remember.

But it's all different now, isn't it? You see the light refracted and remember it goes elsewhere, just as on the three rivers, by the pool in another land. The gods you've heard are here, too, and wonder at this as you drink mineral water and air and drink in the severe beauty of the people who pass, radiating out like the fire infused into coffee, heat slipping through your fingers into the air like their dreams and you suddenly remember how everything fits together.

Meet a friend at an abandoned airfield. Be so full of wonder you fret you cannot hold such happiness, standing where life grows from man's failed plans, gardens and kites and children and old folks playing in a park birthed just as chamomile finds purchase between side-walk cracks. Watch the sun set with your friend, feel his happiness in what others might call sorrow, hope as air, hope as breaks in pavement waiting from life to fill it.

Watch the faces of others watching the sun. Walk towards them, see the violet gold and rose upon their skin, their eyes in wonder, unseeing yours, and know you've seen the same thing with them, and wonder how much life is coursing through you, so much you think you'd break, you'd burn without outlet.

Wanderings

Go get food. It's cheap. You can live off street food here and be well. Wonder why you waited to order, why you prolonged the moments you'd wait in this line, remark to yourself how it probably will mean something to have done so. Listen to the man next to you attempt to order, sense his determination despite his confusion. Smile and help him.

Spend the next couple of hours with him on the street and at a bar where people just ending their night from the day before buy you drinks. Laugh in amusement how it's only 8pm and you're about to go out again, but make plans to take him to the Turks the next day and return home quickly for tea, drink again with that same friend and another, find yourself amongst the pink fur again and smile.

4 October

Tea again, and tomato fennel soup with arugula bruschetta you forged quickly because you woke a bit late and had promised it to your hosts who smile without fret at your tardiness. From scratch, at a cost less than thought possible in that place you're from but you've stopped remarking on this to yourself.

Tea again, and then the lost British boy and the Turkish market and canals and parks and words and words and new wine and dreams. Talk of trees and their meanings, the fourth forfeda's final marks his name, again all weaves together. His wonder at the city reminding you of your wonder, making it a bit easier to integrate, a bit easier to stay calm, a bit easier to fend off what you know is coming.

You know you will return again, but before then you shall go elsewhere. Berlin is a lover who demands nothing and promises nothing, but while you are with him, while you are with her, the world is only always love. Berlin is a home you've never stayed in, though you always may yet you rarely consider it. Berlin is a dream you don't dare manifest, too beautiful to see the light of morning but no-one really sees the light of morning in Berlin except when they leave the bars.

But Berlin isn't the bars, or the sex, or just either. It isn't just the canals and the market and the air. It is this and another thing, a thing you know you cannot plumb, a love you are certain cannot die much more than it can ever fully live.

But see it already on the eyes of someone just here, fumbling with coins to buy a ticket. See the smile in return from your friends, warm acknow-

Your Face Is A Forest

ledgment, their own contentment, their embrace of the same thing you see. And know they all see it, and you are not alone. Stay if you can, leave if you must.

Perhaps it's enough for you to know it is there. Perhaps it is no longer enough for you to know it is there. To know of the gods, or of the ancients, or of the spirits, or of the pyramids temples cathedrals palaces forests springs mountains–it is enough for some. For others it is the end of enough, the death of satedness, and the beginning of everything else

9 October: Fare Forward

I do not have words for the last days of my journey.

This is not to say that they were less wonderful, less fascinating. Playing Breton and Yiddish songs in the smoking room of a club on pause from gay bingo, treading slowly through the press of people in an open-air market to feel their thoughts, sitting wistfully below a willow which for the last three years stood motionless in a framed photograph upon my bedroom wall. Sleeping and waking and dreaming to arms of warmth, smiles of friends unseen for years, the Other whispering always still and then, suddenly, withdrawing until I made a choice.

Staring at a canal from the edge of a bridge, the place I've gone in my head relentless times when the present revealed itself as less than even its shadow, I remembered: it was a vow which brought me here. It will be a vow which brings me back.

You can weave love, like stories, into the warmest of cloaks to wrap about you against the coldest of winds.

Not all shields must be made of wood or metal, and not all which protects you must prevent you.

The night before I left I played in darkness, unknown songs pouring from my flute into the breathing air, the chill. Again, his voice, questioning–"did you forget? You should not forget." Remembered always when most needed, when most required, awakening those who listen past life and death, awakening what hears past flesh and bone.

I'd gone for reasons near numerous as stars, but one, outshining the others, reminded itself to me, what I could not leave without addressing, what I could not part without deciding.

Another vow to gods and land and spirits, another vow to myself.

Wanderings

I have wondered to myself why these nearly five weeks were so different from the other four times I've been to Europe. Each time I've left bits of my soul, bits of my heart in those lands, and have wondered to myself why I'd go back again just to feel the pain of leaving.

Like love, knowing an ending is birthed in every beginning, why embrace what will one day cause pain?

But this analogy falters on a truth I've learned, a self I've finally met. I've scattered myself elsewhere on purpose, to draw myself back, to sabotage the saboteur. I did not know we could wield desire until now, relying only upon unconscious forces and whims to draw ourselves to others, others to ourselves.

I am in America now, after having selected and chosen and left bits of my soul elsewhere for safekeeping, things I intend not to live without, things I must see again.

I once feared promises and oaths, dreams and visions, desire and will. Now I weave a cloak about me, another winter to endure, and I am ever warmed.

In The Forest, A Dream

Everything is love, I think, and we learn this only after we rip apart everything else we build to pave over and hide this awfully embarrassing fact. All the asphalt, the concrete, the towers and walls are there to hide us from death, which is to hide us from love.

Even Death is a sort of love, what waits us all when we tire of hiding from life. Walk through that gate, enter that forest, and you finally begin to live, which is really just beginning to love.

Your Face Is A Forest

Your face is a forest.
There is scruff, yes–bristle like brush, like undergrowth. Hair lined your jaw, like moss on stone or fallen trunk. Thin here, thicker there–a patch missing where stag's antlers sharpened, his scratchings like mine, head grinding against something solid, something yielding just enough against our trying, curious force.

Above, a sense of towering, of shadow which is shade, of branches across which thoughts like animals skittered, jumped and played before hiding again. I watched them dance, then scatter. I followed what I could–they were there, I saw them. Suddenly hidden again, and elsewhere another thought tumbled through bower of needled branch and leaf, and I am distracted still.

Brows overhang pools reflecting the light of grey days, autumnal brooding or spring's pregnant clouds swimming in indifferent certainty through a sky glimpsed through gaps of pine. Past their clouded mirror I could not delve, only listen, watch, drinking carefully at their edges, lapping life fed from unseen fonts deeper than my boots or hoofs could tread.

Your Face Is A Forest

I remember: the wind rose up, shaking your forest with laughter, the soft roar of leaf's response.

I remember: the wind quieted, and I with it, lingering to hear what silence speaks when the world grows still. Gusts which had drawn laughter from leaf and groan from wood had rippled the light and clarity of reflection in those pools; I looked again.

I remember: the image had changed. I stared again, but the silvered-blue dance of life was different, new, another reflection, a new recognition, a new remembering.

I have known forests. I have played to the god of Alder, I've greeted dryads dancing in tassels of Willow. I've lain against Pine, scratched the back of my head against its bark, smelling for days of its sap. At the base of Cedar I collected crimson tears and burned them to meet another. Before a great Spruce fell into a vast ravine, I shared its dreams. I've passed greetings between Maples, I've seen the stars appear to dance on silver-skin of Birch.

But in this forest, I am lost.

I do not remember: am I hunter or stag?
Was I exploring or explored?
I had been one, and then the other, and I am only now remembering what a forest means, what a forest is,

and I am only now remembering I do not know at all.

Donnerlied

I.

Strands of sunlight streaming through the windows of my room, illuminating long shadowed corners. A hot mug of strong ceylon, mildly sweet and milked, thick like coffee, a draught from the well of life.

Ancient music filtered through speakers, reminding of what was and shall be. Wisps of incense rising through the light, filling my mind with scents of elsewhere.

A kind cat companion playing just outside my door amongst the tentative sprouts of my garden, life dancing in life. A lingering chill, clear air breathing like a contented sigh from the quiet mountains.

The presence of gods, whispering patiently, awaiting their revelation. And an anticipation which challenges all my words.

I do not know enough languages to paint for you the serene thrill of an impending presence, a long-awaited visit, a kind haunting of a living soul soon to manifest.

All poetry fails, all prose is just prattle.
Not long. I am happy. I am alive.

Your Face Is A Forest

II.

I have always been proud of my ability to dream fantastic worlds, to envision things more brilliantly illuminated than any light I've seen. Yet sometimes, all dreams prove pale.

Ancient wells overflow in torrents of rain from unseen worlds, and I didn't realise how dry this world had been. Forests overtake vast wastes, mirthful fecundity when I'd been thinking only of a little shade. Overwhelming symphonies scream from the stars when I'd thought only of some simple tune.

I shake my head and smile at how little I'd dared, while Brighid tosses more wood upon the hearth, and laughs.

III.

What is love then, without sorrow? What rain could give more life to the soil of the soul than the tears of parting? From which springs could flow such waters to cleanse the heart, to make it ready for the next embrace?

It is spring. Winter has kept safe all which needed to sleep, has culled from the ground all which needed to die. Now comes to us the awakening, mists falling upon us from the worlds above, from which our lives are seen outside of the time we know.

I have known such joy because of its shadow. I have known the winter which precedes this spring. It is as it must be, world without end.

I am all gratitude. I am all love.

IV.

By the river you were empty, and I was not. We sat on rocks watching geese as we dropped things from pockets, I-- so full of stories I would burst and you without a thing to say. Our boots sloshed rain-soaked muck across our paths, the only sound I recognized.

V.

The note you sometimes read, falling from the pages of the book you finally filled with ink, the stone, probably covered with feathers, snakeskin and leaves. They are like the words I read now, the words I write now, etched in moss-covered stone settling in for another winter.

It is never long until the next spring.

Our Sister

There is nothing so beautiful in the world as the rising of the moon over mountains, reflected upon a lake as you greet it, except knowing that it reflects that light upon all those you love, close by or very far from you.

I would be the light upon that face

I would the face that reflects such light

I would be the myriad stars wheeling about her

And the myriad dreams under her gaze.

The Sword Pointed At The Heart

I once heard some pop-pysch pablum state that depression is merely anger turned inward. But ignore the source, and consider the consequences of passivity in the face of oppression. Ridiculous work conditions, societies formed to maintain poverty, increasingly territory of the self claimed as a field of commerce. Ask for a raise, get denied, sing a Smith's song in your head ("you just haven't earned it yet, baby/you must suffer and apply for another time.") Or rail a bit about your boss to friends or family, or slack off, steal some office supplies, but in the end, accept.

Watch the cost of food rise slowly at the grocery store. Eat a little less, purchase lower quality food, cut into your savings, decline to go out on that date because you don't want to admit you're a bit too poor.

Walk past 20 people who ask you for change, or a cigarette. Decline each, or every person after the first. Shake your head, entertain notions that they're not really poor, or get a little angry that they're asking you and not someone else, or push your headphones in closer.

Hear news that the tipping point on global warming has been reached, another species is endangered, there's some war somewhere or other. Go home and drink, or smoke weed and try to forget. Or watch a movie and try to forget.

In The Forest, A Dream

Vote, though you know it doesn't do a thing. Exercise, because at least you've got your body. Do yoga, or meditate, or pray as the people die from economic sanctions, or proxy wars, or remote-controlled planes, or manufactured famines.

Know something's wrong, but know you can't live angry, because anger makes you want to do things, and there's safety in inaction.

Read the histories, if you dare. The slaves which built this land up from the rivers of blood of systematic slaughter. Know that the same thing happened elsewhere, maybe to your own people. Shrug, or worse–let your ancestral suffering justify that of others.

See the angry throngs in other lands, but dismiss them because they are not white, or they don't have computers and grocery stores. But know this isn't enough for you–swallow the fear and sympathy, try to digest that feeling and wonder why you feel ill, why the sun seems sallow.

Inherit memories from yourself. Remember the rejection each time you tried or the conflict each time you spoke. Inherit that pain and blame yourself. You are not good enough. You are too weak. You are not enough.

Hear the voices of the gods speak, and throw their whispers back at them, pretend it's all echo, all madness. You can change nothing, because to change a thing is to assert a self into the world and it's safer to have no self at all.

Confront the dead, their memories, the torment and dislocation and sorrow and try to convince yourself there's nothing you can do any longer. The world is not yours, you are but no one, you are nothing in the face of so much potential for rage.

Stare dumbly at the sword in your hands and consider asking yourself why you've had the point aimed at your heart your entire life.

The Sighted & The Blind

There's something here.

I'd woken early, on purpose, though early for me is still much later for most. Rode my bike to a coffeeshop, groggy; rode my bike back one handed, sipping the hot liquid, still groggy.

There's something here. Look around.

Groggy. Have stuff to do. Bike loaded on the bus. So much to do before work. I've been working too much for weeks–excess judged not on having too much money (or even enough), but from having too little time to do what I need to do. Work, I guess, is a need, or the money derived from it is a need, but there's the other stuff, the writing, the forest, the candles, the dreaming, the last bits of my late garden, the friends, the sewing, the crafting, but most of all the gods and spirits.

No. This wasn't a mistake. Give attention.

In The Forest, A Dream

I do Social Work. You don't really *work* as a social worker, you *do Social Work*. It spills over into the rest of your life; to do it, you have to train yourself to understand any sort of uncomfortable person, the very violent wielding-a-knife-at-you sort probably just needs to talk something out, the hasn't-taken-a-shower-in-months sort may have a putrefying skin condition that she's ashamed to look at and so won't take off her clothes, the screaming-incoherently-in-a-sing-song-voice may actually be telling you that they were just raped if you can solve their riddle.

It spills over, builds on what empathy you had for others and constructs great "walls of caring" or "towers of sympathy" around what's good about you, great fortresses from which you can then launch assaults against human misery and suffering without being destroyed yourself.

It spills over too much sometimes, drenching the rest of your life in too-much awareness. Your life changes. Friends who want to tell you about a television show they watched become meaningless. Companions who step over homeless people on the street become empty shells of humanity. You can no longer unsee the suffering in others.

This is very strange. Go the way you intended

You get tools, though. Discipline. You shake off the violence from a difficult shift, you sit a little while with the sorrow of a client death, you burn a little extra incense after smelling too many bacterial infections. You avoid places where your clients will be when you're not at work. You set boundaries when you pass by them–I'm not on the clock, I can't help you right now. You don't want to do this–you don't want to see them about to get arrested for public urination or inebriation, but you must.

You start to get grumpy when you realize no-one else around them is helping them. And then your friends call you, asking for help, too. You have several client deaths in a week and you can't look at another human being and yet a friend's brother said he wants to die, or someone's getting kicked out of their apartment and they want to know what their rights are. You can't not help them, even though you're exhausted. Much of your week was spent doing the same thing, using up all that kindness for others, but maybe there's still a little left for those you love.

He can't see.

Your Face Is A Forest

Groggy, confused. Wrong bus stop. How'd that happen? Composing a message to a friend, distracted. I've been so focused lately, though tired. I'm hungry, I have to go to work, I have to scan a confirmation so I can go to Newgrange, I really need more incense, I need to make more candles, I could really use a beer, I wish I could call off sick.

How'd it get this way? I'm always writing when I'm not working. I'm often writing while working, in those spaces in-between when no-one requires my attention. And then home, more writing, a video conversation with my lover who's too far away right now. Prayers at the altar. New gods are arriving, new spirits introduced. Great gifts, great kindnesses, new Mysteries.

I'm running out of room on my altar. I need beer for some. The mead I made is running low. The candle I made is near burnt-out. This enchanted water here, that vow there. Things required of me because I offered, and I like to keep promises.

So tired, but this fatigue's been strange. A month of my lover, and now he's gone for awhile, and I almost didn't notice I've been mourning his absence. Also, I haven't eaten much.

He's gonna walk into traffic.

It's the same oath to all of them, a simple one. One that I know I can fulfill, though it's open enough that it can mean more than what either of us intended. It's alright. They give gifts to help.

I was warned. Fuck, was I warned. Over and over again a friend who knew these things told me to beware. They'll take everything you have, he'd tell me. You'll be theirs. Your life won't be the same.

The warnings only made me more eager.

He walked into a wall, and now he's gonna try to cross a street?

I know what I was isn't what I am now, though I can barely trace the changes. I used to be a lot more scared. I used to worry that sometimes I wasn't attractive. I used to dig my bare fingers into garden soil and keep them there sometimes because it was all too much.

That was all before, but the garden soil is a really good idea.

When's the last time I played a video game? Watched a movie and didn't see its relationship to something else? When did I last sleep-in on purpose?

In The Forest, A Dream

How long has it been since I saw a tree and thought it was "only a tree?" What was it like when I didn't notice every crow calling on the street or outside my house? What am I going to do with all the rocks and feathers I've gathered?

I forgot what it's like not to notice where the wind's coming from, or to have an inconsequential fuck. What was it like to feel despair in a place and not want to figure out who had caused it, or to feel great joy in another place and not want to leave some gift?

What was it like to fear the dead, to fear death? What was it like not to even think on the dead at all?

He'll never find it. Help him.

When you first meet the gods, it's pretty intense. I'd throw poetry at you to describe this, but that's mostly what I've been doing this entire time. And my words are part of my oath to them, that I'd use my words for them.

You get used to the trauma. Brighid and Brân were pretty calm, though Brân's been the only one who actually got physical with me. Arianrhod and Ceridwen were pretty dark, and also fiercely bright. Dionysos (I've said this before) has been a wild fucking ride, and that's not just me being profane.

The Morrighan? I do not talk about this, except to say that I don't think we'll be working with each other much, except when there's some overlapping need of another with mine.

Maponus lingered, was there and gone. Apollo shouted "don't fuck this up" at me, I guess. Hestia seemed bothered by the trouble. Hecate's like this big wheel of mysterious gifts that make no sense at all which I need every time and wouldn't have thought to ask and never really know what to do with. And then there's others, lingering, others waiting for me to have the time.

The land spirits have been awesome, except when they're angry, and they speak even less like humans than the gods, and so it's all confusion followed by picking up litter.

The dead, though? That almost broke me.

He's blind, and this is new. He doesn't know how to do this. He can't see the path, or the cars, or the–

Your Face Is A Forest

The man asked me how to find the hospital and I told him. He wasn't far, a brief walk up a hill or an even briefer bus. Take the 60, I told him. It goes right there.

I watched him walk towards the stop, his balance off. Drunk, perhaps, though I hadn't smelled it on his breath. Attractive. Looks a bit like my lover, dressed like a professor.

I don't know why I'm at this bus-stop. It was the wrong stop, a mistake I never make. And I'm rooted in place, confused, trying to fight off this sense that I'm missing something.

It's the sense you get when five people say the same thing in the space of a few hours, a reference to bees, or some domestic task, or something about loud birds, or their dreams. There's some pattern there, but you don't know it, can't find it, can't be certain you're not a little mad.

I can't move from where I am, I'm so confused. It's this voice.

This is important. Give attention. There he is again. He won't make it. Why'd you get off the wrong stop? Why are you here?

I told him how to get to the bus, and I watched him take a different one, one that I needed. It was a bit far, I wouldn't catch it, but maybe I could.

I caught it, because he was still fumbling with change to pay the driver when I got there. He'd inadvertently held it for me, saving me time.

I loaded my bike, sat down, took out my phone. A bad habit, one I loathe, one I try to avoid. I try to be open to the world around me, to hear the outside rather than listening to the inside.

I look up, and he's gotten off the bus, and he walks into a wall.

You trust us yet?

I think spirit-work and god-work might be best when it's like Social Work, and sometimes I can't tell the difference. A god needs something done, and so you help. A person wants to meet a god, and so you do what you can to help this. A forest is in pain, or a spirit is troubled, and so you try to make this better. Just like "normal" life, if you've got your eyes open, if you're not cowering in fear of the 'other' or locked up in your car or wealth.

It bleeds out into everything else. You meet people who treat the gods like they don't matter and you feel a kind of internal despair, just as when

In The Forest, A Dream

you watch someone step over a homeless kid. You hear someone say they don't really exist, and it's in the same voice as those who say the poor should just get jobs.

You try to let it go, but you cannot always. This is what you do, now, but there's something else we forget to mention. It becomes, in retrospect, what you always wanted to do.

Working for and with the dead, and the land spirits, and the gods becomes a fulfillment of all that you'd been trying to do anyway. You're not transmuted, you're made more yourself. Unlike the Christian's God, they don't cleanse you of all that was bad or fun or broken. You're not "fixed," because there's nothing to fix. Just some stuff that could use a polish or a tweaking, a few things you really ought to have gotten over by now, and a profound sense that you can never go back.

But I never want to.

Good. Thanks. He needed that. So did you.

He'd just gone blind from some viral infection. It was sudden, and he was trying to get to the hospital. He couldn't see more than a few feet in front of him, and he didn't know Seattle, because he was from somewhere else.

I'd given him directions that he couldn't follow because he couldn't see.

Took me a little while to notice he was lost. Took me a little while to notice he would not find his way.

He may have made it, but that's not even a question I can ask. He found his way because I guided him

For him, directions were not enough. A companion, a voice–someone who knew the way, someone who could figure out what might be needed. It only took noticing–

–like it takes noticing to find a forest no one sees, to weave threads between events and events, to stitch tattered theories and misplaced theologies into a tapestry of meaning. This is the work of a mage, the song of a bard, the lust of a priest, the love of a radical.

Where They May Be Found

You can stare at a line of trees in front of you and never notice there's a forest behind them, just as you can look for love with all your being and not notice that it's the very substance of your being.

I wanted to find gods. I wrote in a journal, years ago, that I really wished they actually existed still. I never doubted that they probably had at one point, because there's no point doubting what people used to believe.

It seemed as if there'd been a great hole, an Abyss, through which all the meaning had once leaked out of the world, and the most I could hope for was to find that hole to be certain it was all merely gone, not just lost.

And then—well, yeah. They never left.

Here's where I find them.

Brân

While Trying to Go To A Shrine

I'm walking home from work. It's a bit chill, early March in Seattle, that city blessed of so much rain that only a writer can really endure its winters without complaining, the sky so close to the earth. People talk of blue skies as if "blue" means clear; sodden from the perpetual dripping of rain from that city's cavernous ceiling, I knew deeply that grey is composed of every blue.

Trudging, actually, up the tree-flanked streets. To climb those hills without faltering, you must step as if on stairs. Wearing boots helps, though not to keep out the puddles, only to tone the calves upon those ascents. I guess you could maybe drive, but cars are for people who don't like streets or trees and so must zoom past them quickly to get away from them.

It is nothing to sit on a stone bench in the rain in such a city, if you've been there long enough. This was my intention, white benches describing part of the circle-shrine where I and others sometimes prayed. It was to the Mother of God, and she seemed sometimes almost to intercede for us for other gods, though I think this was only my hope, not the truth. I tried to walk to the shrine, and suddenly felt a hard push stop me.

Your Face Is A Forest

I tried again, and the push was harder. A third time, and I gave up (I used to give up easily, I remember). And then a voice, the sort somewhere between the ears and the head, "tonight you meet another god."

While On The Isle of Ravens and Alder

I'm with my best friend, the man who taught me to feed the crows. He moved three blocks from my house so we never needed to walk very far for tea, and the walk between us was littered with crow feathers. He's in Wales now, which is too long of a walk for tea.

We're camping in a rainforest. If you've not been to the Northwest, you may be thinking "jungle." That's not where we were, because neither of us like the heat. We were in the Hoh.

Sometimes ancient things are beautiful, and sometimes they are terrifying. Sometimes in Berlin and Strasbourg I would walk home from bars rather drunk and suddenly turn a cobbled-corner and see a 900 year old Cathedral and shout "older than shit!" at it because it was beautiful and terrifying. The Hoh Rainforest is like this.

We're camped near the river, which is also very old and very beautiful and extremely cold, and there's an island out there that you can get to only by fording across or climbing a fallen tree. I've got no balance to speak of, neither on river rocks nor fallen trees, so such quandaries terrify me more than old cathedrals and ancient Spruce.

I got across. I'm not sure why I took off my clothes, except that they were probably wet. There were no other humans to see me, and I'm comfortable being nude with non-humans because they generally don't stare too intently, but I cannot really say that I'm certain the ravens which circled weren't watching.

I played my wooden recorder, first to the river, then the island, then the circling ravens and then the vast assemblage of Red Alder which seemed to crowd the banks of the river. And I was playing to someone else, but wasn't sure he liked that sort of thing, but then I realized he did.

Afterwards, I wandered around the trails through caverns of moss and trees older than cathedrals holding an elk tooth in my hand. I smeared salmonberries on the elk tooth, because it seemed like the right thing to do. And then I found myself in a grove of Alder, and they seemed to crowd around me, and they gave me something to take with me.

Not until the journey back to Seattle from the rainforest did I read that Brân is a god of Alder, and I'd forgotten what islands mean to him.

Where They May Be Found

Where Men Play By Water and Willow

It's Lugnasadh. I'm grumpy. I'd tried to get four other gay druids together for a ritual and failed. It hasn't nothing to do with us being gay, but it amuses me that we all were.

So instead I'm sitting on a peninsula near an abandoned off-ramp on Lake Washington. It's marshy and post-apocalyptic and serene except I forgot that it's near a popular gay cruising spot. Gay men often like to have sex in really sacred places (in fact, if you're looking for land spirits, such places are a great place to start), and I'm sitting in a circle of Willow hoping that I can be invisible, and hoping that no-one would try to pick-up the grizzled witchy-looking guy with all the candles and incense and feathers and books amongst the willows.

It's not going well. A man has just walked through my circle and I want to rip him apart, but he's actually really nice and besides I'd just asked for a guide for this gate and he doesn't seem to be trying to cruise me. He apologizes, and goes off and sits with his book looking out on the water, and then suddenly gets up, returns to the edge of my circle, and tells me a story.

"In two weeks," he says, "I'll have been married 25 years. My wife is taking me to a small island in Alaska where we first met." And he's got tears in his eyes, happy tears, and he's so in love it almost hurts to look at because I'm not in love at the moment, and so I don't know why I'm doing this but I hand him a raven feather and say, "hey. When you go to that island, leave this feather there. It's a good thing to do." And he thanks me, like I've just blessed his marriage, and assures me he will and then the visions start flooding in and all I can see is what Brân's trying to show me.

Other Places

You can stand on top of a mountain in Bretagne and see him, and also see the small chapel where he's around like crazy, especially in the black-and-crimson woodwork, and I don't know why those are his colors.

But that's Europe, and that's also a far walk for tea, like Wales, where he was worshiped.

You can meet him in dreams, especially when you're standing at gates. Or at the base of a tower in a park where you're about to play recorder and then an empty crow's egg falls on you. I think if you feed the crows or ravens, you might get a slightly better glimpse. You can cross a river to an

Your Face Is A Forest

island which is also a gay cruising spot on the Willamette with your really cool friend who's writing a story and then, on your way back to the shore, have your guide who doesn't know anything of the gods suggest you "lay yourself down across the river and let her walk across you."

Or you can be standing outside work on a break, thinking about how you're gonna write something about Brân, and then a crow feather falls at your feet, and all the crows cackle and laugh and wheel around you as you bike home. And laugh a bit when you get off your bike to look at this really strange and particularly beautiful spot along the creek and finally notice you're in front of a very old Alder.

Stand at the base of stone towers, or be really quiet in a stand of alders, or feed the crows and watch them dance, or ford a stream to an island, or give a feather to someone in love and call out to him. Just keep in mind that your call might actually be your reply.

Arianrhod

"We are all in the gutter, but some of us are looking at the stars."
–Oscar Wilde

In What Earth Sees of Sky

I was once told by a man in a dream to look for the gods in the rain, and what's in-between the rain. But I don't meet Arianrhod in the rain, but what's before and what's after.

A decade ago I began staring at puddles again. Ever done this? Since you were a kid, I mean, playing in the little lakes upon stone, pooling water from rains standing still as glass until you stomp them? When I was really young, I'd watch the wind ripple their surface and imagined they were strange silver coins, there and gone.

The Welsh word for money is Arian, which is the word for silver.

When you stare at a puddle, you see yourself reflected, but it is a different sort of mirror. I once foolishly imagined we had no mirrors before mirrors, and then remembered that we've always had still water on stone. We've always been able to look down past our feet into the world as seen from the earth, what we'd look like if stone had eyes like ours.

Your Face Is A Forest

You can see yourself, shadowy but there, an image I suspect closer to "truth" than the ones we see in polished surface. When I feel unwell, or lost in the world, I stare at myself like this and smile. But I'm not the only vision in the water, and never the most interesting.

She's on the surface, and I don't know how this works. She's what becomes of the sky in water, silver and blue like the Kingfisher. The sky before storms, the sky after storms, so many blues that people just shrug and call it grey.

Above A Meadow, Amongst Chamomile

The last night in Bretagne, end of three months traveling with another. After the festival on the Rhine where the wind swirled mist from the surface of the river into spirals of air-and-water, where sailors meet the arms of the Rhine's daughter. After two weeks in the medieval city. That night before the night before we'd return, we took a train to Rennes to say goodbye.

Tired. Our place taken. Only a field left in which to camp. Raining (and you learn to distrust the rain when camping, despite its beauty). Just some grass and
 and
 and a
And a broken beautiful screaming sky, every blue and violet and rose and, and, and gold and over and over again and that
 arcing dancing silver.

We watched for hours in the wet grass and didn't hold back the tears and couldn't understand why we smelled chamomile until we gathered so many blossoms for our last tea there and, oh,

That dream.

In Dreams When You Are Not Asleep

Light on a river refracts into patterns so hypnotic you almost disappear and find yourself there, suddenly. Elsewhere. Electricity is too simple, too banal and human to describe the celestial sense, but it's the only cognate I know.

When I think of the gods receding from our view because of what we've done with the earth's blood, the petty uses into which we channel such power, I think of her receding, walking backwards into the ocean towards her isle, disappointed.

Where They May Be Found

She's in dreams, strange blue-and-silver dreams. An owl, its feathers dripping in chemical fire like the phoenix, flying towards me just after I met another god. She was somewhere in the court of that castle where I got my name, because I'm pretty certain it was her castle.

And then there are all the other women around her, not her I now know but women who serve her, and sometimes they appear and more often than not seem disappointed in me. Not upset, I don't think. Usually just "oh. You forgot again? You're always forgetting."

I am always forgetting.

I am always forgetting to look up just before and after sunset when her colors are everywhere.

I am always forgetting to look down at what springs through pavement, what pools there, and what it sees.

I am too often forgetting to look up after dark, outside amongst the trees, the stars wheeling endlessly above.

Where Stars Dance, Just Before Death, Just Before Life

The sky is a sea, the sea's skin the reflection of sky. Light from one to another, light so far and hot like the candle flame–yellow and red but look closer at the source and see the color it starts as.

Stars are balls of flaming gas if animals are mere food and trees are mere fuel, humans mere workers and puddles mere bits of water.

When I first heard the phrase "the music of the spheres" I got terrified, because I'm pretty sure it was that alien sound I'd heard in silence as a child, not the ringing of tinnitus but that electric–no, pre-electric, or what electric wants to be but cannot because it only powers human-things, not every-being things–that, sound.

I've heard that silence and noticed what I couldn't hear but tried to hear and the strain tires so much you cannot imagine sleeping, what the stars are saying, what the stars are singing.

Ariadne's Crown is Arianrhod's Castle. This isn't a mistake, but it also isn't a simple She is She, anymore than I am you. And if we're standing, you and I, under those stars long enough, they wheel about us even as the earth wheels below us, and somehow in the same, the correspondence but not equivalence, she is there, receding like the tide, surging like the floods, singing like the stars.

Stare past the reflection at what you can't see without it. Cry for what is lost even as it returns to drown you in those stars. And call her name, but know you may need a new one of your own.

Cernunnos

 I actually don't know where He's found, but I took a man hunting for him. Actually, how do you hunt a god? You don't, really. They hunt you. Or maybe you hunt them as the hunted hunt the hunter, or haunt the hunter.
 I don't know much about Cernunnos. Others do, and have some awfully good recommendations on how to find Him. I've only seen him once, maybe twice. It's strange to write about a god you don't know personally and tell others where he might be found. Mayhaps even presumptuous.
 It's all presumption, though, isn't it? I go to places and see gods and presume that you'd want to meet Them. I'm not actually certain why you wouldn't, but I'm sure there are probably good reasons.
 Or maybe, if you haven't met them, you feel a bit outside, a bit dubious. I get that. I feel a bit outside of this, particularly. Cernunnos isn't "my god." There's no shrine to him on my altar, and only perhaps the leaves I've gathered from strange places and the elk tooth I carried in my hands through the forest to represent him.

Where They May Be Found

On the Face of Another, in a Forest

See, my companion lives in a desert and worships a forest god. In fact, he hadn't seen much of forests, and it made an awful lot of sense and seemed like a grand thing to take him through some while he visited me. Who wouldn't want to take a beautiful man for a walk through the trees to the craggy top of an urban mountain? And besides, I love the man, and forests walks with lovers–oh, you get the point.

I heard someone sing about Cernunnos once. I was at a festival with two friends. One wore a wolf-mask crafted by a fellow writer, the other a beaked avian mask, and I wore mine, blue-green-gold draconic-canine face.

We're there, and a band is doing awkward and violent hip-thrusts evoking animalistic sex and saying something about Cernunnos and it doesn't feel right. Actually, it feels awful.

I'd only met one god by then, and she's not known for hip-thrusts, but still–it felt like there wasn't a god there at all. In fact, if the musicians were correct about Him, I found myself wanting to have very little to do with him.

It wasn't him, though.

I saw him once in a vision a few months after that, right around the time I was having more visions than I could really handle. He was huge, indifferent, waiting, and utterly impatient with crowds of drunken revelers copulating as obeisance. He threw them off, violently, like the earth shaking off cities built along faults or vacation homes nestled in drought-stricken California woodlands.

For awhile I thought I'd seen Dionysos, instead, but that was cleared up later. I'll tell you where I've found him another time.

Have you ever seen the face of a man seeing a river for the first time? Climbing out onto water along the fallen trunk of a still-living Willow, following the patterned leaves of unfamiliar, northern trees, staring at a wild bee-hive, hearing a summering wind shake the branches of Birch and Maple as the sun filters across his face?

May you one day have that chance.

In the Face of The Forest, on Another

I like trees and forests and the wilds, but the gods I worship are mostly associated with the places we dwell. Very wild places are no longer wild when you visit them, because by "wild" we mean "without humans," or

Your Face Is A Forest

"nature without a specific part of nature." Funny how that works, huh? We've the fantasy of being out in the wilds, "alone" in nature. The sight of another human on a trail disturbs the fantasy, of course, but if we're wise (and I'm not very often wise), we'd remind ourselves the family passing us through the pristine wild belongs there no less than we do.

Cities are full of Nature, because they're composed of Nature's denizens. The non-urban forests, though–yeah. That's where you'll find him.

We sat under an Alder together by a stream and watched as a leaf sailed several meters against the current to land at my companion's feet. "It's for you," I told him, because it was, because you learn to notice those things, even when you don't actually have much to do with the powers working such things. He accepted the stream's gift, and I left with as much wonder as he.

We climbed to the top of the highest point in Eugene. I'd promised I'd show him trees, and he saw them, stretched out for miles in all directions. We kissed there, and elsewhere, but though I'd acted as his guide out of love, I'd also offered this to Cernunnos. Yeah, we don't talk really, but he seems rather awesome, and it was an easily-proffered service. "I'll show one of your devotees what I can," I'd said, an act of worship I give also to my gods, which is partially why I'm writing all this for you.

I can't say for certain precisely where Cernunnos was, but I could tell he was there, or everywhere, the way the wind rose up just as we neared the end of our path through the trees, the spinning falling Maple leaves dancing horizontal across our view, the speckled slug collecting dried pine needles upon its slimed body, the deep feeling of happiness in my hand which clutched the berry-smeared elk-tooth, and, most of all, the look on my companion's face, seeing the face of the forest

Ceridwen

Maybe you know the story. A goddess had two children: one beautiful, one hideous. And because she knew that beauty didn't really matter all that much, or because she knew that it only mattered to others, that it was a way to elicit attention from others, to get others to think you worth their time, she decided she'd give her son wisdom.

She could have given him power, or wealth, the usual substitutes for beauty. With money he could have maybe afforded braces so that he'd look like what everyone else thought they looked like, with freakishly straight rows of horse-teeth like those seen in the glossy magazines. Or he could buy a large SUV with tinted windows so no-one could see his face, or he could invest so much into advertisements for clothing and self-care products that people would spend so much time worrying about how ugly they felt that they wouldn't notice his hideous disfigurement.

Or power. Her son could have put his detractors to death, or made them work forty hours a week for him at very low wages. Maybe he could have made them feel lazy for needing to go to the bathroom, or made them fear for their survival if they asked for a lunch break. He could maybe have bombed their countries into oblivion, or made them run, terrified, out of the crosswalk because he didn't want to wait for a light.

But no. She thought wisdom would be a better fit.

Your Face Is A Forest

In the Place Where You Are Already Dead

I bought a cauldron at an herbalist shop run by people who did not notice it was a cauldron. They called the cast iron bowl with four feet and a handle an "aromatherapy base." The perplexed and disturbed look upon their faces, in their yoga-pants and earth tones, when I called it a "cauldron" made me feel very, very alone.

It was small, but it weighed on me as I walked home to the place that wasn't my home any longer, the house full of ghosts of loves and friends, the place I'd lived and dreamed but now didn't belong. In a few weeks I would leave everything I knew, put the cauldron and everything else I could carry into my rucksack and camp, alone in Europe until I found what I wasn't certain I could find.

I couldn't go back yet, couldn't bear the dying present. Though it was late summer, everything felt cold, the clear night sky lightening a little just as the moon began to rise. So I walked, down streets and alleys I did not know anymore, gazing at the life and light behind blinds and curtains, families gathered for dinner or before flickering blue-lit screens. I walked as a ghost, unmarked, unnoticed, feeling the weight of the iron in my pack so much heavier with each step, its blackness an abyss that wanted to swallow me.

And then the moon rose, her moon, the sharpest of sickles, the gold-then-pale crescent blade. It seemed it would blood me, and yet I no longer feared death. Every moment is death, which is why every moment is also life.

Atop the Dredged Swamp, Surrounded By Asphalt, As The Seas Rise

This is not an easy thing.

When I was young, I would ask my mother what happened to all the children who drowned in the tub.

It must not have been easy for a woman with latent schizophrenia stranded in an Appalachian shack with three children and a violent husband to hear her son ask this question There were no such children--but I remember them. There were children, and then their mother drowned them. They were kin to me, and I mourned them, even though they didn't exist in this life. I was first-born--there were no others before me, and yet I remember them, still.

Where They May Be Found

I don't know why I remember them like this, nor why I, so otherwise hostile to the macabre, have always been fascinated with stories of mothers who drown their children, one after another, in bathtubs.

Decades later, my sister and I finally find a seat in deli surrounded by asphalt and SUVs in a South Florida city. We're probably the only ones who haven't just come from church, the only ones who have ever used food assistance.

My sister's telling me about a friend we once knew, wealthy beyond our own comprehension, now with his sixth child. And I'm unable to stop myself thinking on six children growing up, each getting their own house in the dredged swamplands of south Florida, two or three stories, air conditioned, each with their own massive vehicles and more asphalt laid down upon the dying wetlands to make room for them and all the others like them, and I'm telling my sister all this and then I hear Her voice, somewhere between mirth and rage:

"Understand, then, why I drown children."

Everywhere There Is Life, Because There Is Death

We consume the dead. Grains and vegetables ripped from their umbilical roots, flesh carved from still-bleeding beasts who looked dumbly at the assassin's blade. We feast on death, fell trees to build our homes and wipe our asses. The black blood and stone we rip from the womb of the earth were once flesh and fiber of forests we wouldn't recognize, creatures we can't comprehend, and we burn it to run our cars and turn on our lights. Each new thing is birthed from death, and at the beginning of each life is the coming of its end.

She had two faces when I saw her. Living, fleshed, stern, unfathomable. The other, the face of death. And I did not know she could look so kind.

To know each beautiful thing must die is not easy. Each love will end, each laugh trail off into silence. My words will one day cease, my eyes grow finally dark. His smile, her laughter, their joy, our sorrow–it all shall one day feed others.

Look, there, into the abyss, the blackness of the cauldron. Contemplate the only thing which can stop our hunger. See the death in everything which sustains life, and see her face smiling back, see why She chose wisdom as her gift, why love is like death, and why death is how we know of love.

Brighid

In a Barn, With Queers, With Curry

I have dreamt more on Brighid than I quite know how to understand.

Once, I was in a wooden hovel. Herbs hung from rafters, and I was cooking, but I was not me, but her. Or, rather, I was there on her behalf, and I was cooking for people full of lustful desire for each other and others. An odd dream, one I never fully understood.

And then a little more than a year later, I was standing in a barn, cooking. It was the place in the dream, but it was larger, and the herbs were on shelves, too, and dried flowers hung from the rafters, as did a swing.

It was an odd place, and I was cooking for people on Beltane, and they were quite the lusty sort. Two hundred or so of them, and I'm making curry, and I know why I'm doing it. I hadn't intended to, but there was no one else, and I once ran kitchens and catered, and anyway it was her.

The moment before I started, I knew. The moment after it ended, I told them all it was on her behalf, and theirs.

More than any god I've thus far met, she's woven through the moment of service, food to the hungry, homes to the homeless.

Where They May Be Found

Between Home and Home

And on that matter, I have many times been homeless, and I left a home for her.

Camping by ancient ruins is fantastic, but it is a bit harder when you know you're carrying your home with you. I had a home, but I knew it was not where I would stay, where my journey would end.

There's a story about Brighid and a druid. It might seem the story is more about the druid than her, but I do not think this is true.

In this story, a Druid's son-in-law has no land for his new wife. He asks the druid for wisdom from Brighid about the matter. The druid asks, and she answers: "the land of the first person he asks will be his." The son-in-law, hearing this, demands from the druid all his land, and the druid, knowing her words, gives it to him.

She is like this, yes. It was she whom I first met, before a hearth, laughing. And it was on account of her that I left. It was not like this story, yet also very much like this story.

The druid left his home with all his possessions, traveling endlessly without a home because of a goddess of the hearth. I don't remember how long they traveled, and I do not remember what else the druid was said to have found along the way. But he came finally to a place that would be his home again.

In the Laughter of Firelight, the Whisper of Candlelight

She is a goddess of the hearth. There are some who think of Her also of the forge. And I think of Her, also, as an Alchemist

In the fires of the hearth, water and vegetables and bones transmute to stew; in the flames of the forge, metals from the earth become tools. We separate and combine through fire to create. What was becomes what is now, something new from what was old.

I suspect she does the same.

The "waste" product of heat is light. Heat combusts the life of the earth, and from it we are able to see. Stars and the sun give off light from internal alchemy, and by this we are able to live.

Your Face Is A Forest

The flame which consumes the candle whispers voicelessly, but you can see its dance upon the wick.

She is, I think, the easiest to find of the gods. By streams and wells, by caves, in kitchens. In the light of a candle, the warmth of a fire, the ferocity of the sun. I didn't need to visit a mountain where she was worshiped to find her, but I learned there where else to look.

Light burns, and fire creates. In even sorrow, there is mirthful laughter. Tend to the flames by which we see each other, tend to the lights which never go out. Bring others out from the cold. Remember why desire must be fed, and why some things must be burnt to the ground, why Brighid tosses more wood upon her hearth, and laughs.

Dionysos

Under Pine, Pining

Behind words are other words. Hidden, shadowed meanings, dancing in the edges we imagine are solid, like the borders between realms. The closer to the boundried contours of the word and not the word, definition slips. Define a word, de-fine, show us its edges, its limits, its end.

A word means another word, but what means *means*? What is the meaning of meaning? What does meaning mean?

I'm not playing with you, but play with me, play with this if you've time. Long, maybe not too long.

You've longed, yeah? Long isn't short, but long is what, precisely?

And you've longed, of course. For how long have you longed? For a man, a woman, an other, a fragment of yourself or the world or the Other, found that you are suddenly stretched out but not flattened.

Expanded, pulled towards even as you incline towards, but not pulled away. You long, and the hours grow long though others tell you that they are the same length, and therein's why science isn't poetry.

Longing under pine. He's there (I mean He's there), but He's also not there, because he's not here, not there with you. You long. You pine. Your soul expands as the sky grows dark, as Her stars filter through needles, the

Your Face Is A Forest

smell of sap wakening something more luscious, more intoxicating, than sleep.

It's an ache, but it's one you cling to, embrace, coddle and protect and nurture. He was said to be sewn into the leg of a god, an ache to be nurtured. But the ache isn't that it's there, it's that it's not there yet still there, inside you, the place he left, the place you made for him, the place he carved from you, the place

He inhabits.

When you pine against the bark of a pine, the sap clings to you, like his scent when he's gone, haunting like the gods. And somewhere, not far, between the longing and the pining, He's there.

In Desire, Dancing

Sweat drips off the chest in the languid summer heat, the close space, matted hair and fur and laughter. Saltwater drips from pores and you pour some to Him, crimson vine-blood. Satyrs dance in the forest, just out of sight of firelight, but you're not in a forest at all.

You can dance in a forest, but who else would be there? You can also dance in a forest, if you desire.

You can desire in other forests, forests inside, forests filled with satyrs who are men, nymphs who are women, and men-who-are-women or were women and women-who-are-men or were men or will be, and every body in-between.

Dancing, but not dancing. Whirling like Her stars, or standing still. A crown in the heavens, a wheel, a dance.

Dance mimics desire. Dance is desire. Desire is a dance, between yourself and an other, an other and you. Every other, every you, and every Other.

Watch him dance. Watch her dance. Watch Them dancing as they dance, know there's an Other there, and many throngs of Others.

Dionysos is rarely alone.

Amidst the Dead Who Laugh With You

Actually, you were crying.

Actually, you weren't, or were but are not. You thought you were alone, but you were not. You thought they were gone, but they aren't. He's gone, but He's back. Why do they go away?

Why does He go away?

Where They May Be Found

He's elsewhere, and you stop asking why, because He comes back, even as She came back, or went elsewhere. Most mostly stay, are there when you pour out to them what you offer, are there to tell you something, to warn, to request. Sometimes just to remind you They're there.

He, though. Where's He go? It doesn't matter, because you know Others are with Him, laughing. He's with Him, and she, and you hear them sometimes, laughing, passing through.

I heard them in a tavern, not long ago, while longing, while pining. I didn't expect them. No one asks when you pour the first part of your drink onto the floor and hail Him. You'd think they would, but then you remember that they are remembering, for a moment, where they are.

And then He comes through, but you don't notice Him first. You hear them, the Dionysian dead. They're playing and shaping the laughter around you as you watch, sober, writing in a journal at the bar, waiting.

Gods, they're loud, and welcome.

Everyone's laughing, and the dead shaped their mirth, give depth to their revelry. So loud you can't mistake it, so loud you look again at your full drink just to make sure.

And then gone, just like the living.

Where did the dead go?

Where do the living go?

Some go with Him.

In the Seething Madness of Those You've Ignored

Eleutherios.

Liberator.

They're coming for you. Burning barricades, broken glass, hurled cobbles, shattered chains.

There's some Guédé who've got something to say about what you've done, and some Barons, too. Some dragged-out masked punks seething with rage. Angry immigrants sick of scraps, seething nymphs and feral satyrs gonna rip you to shreds.

Ripping off chains you put on 'em, 'cause chains ain't just iron.

Howling madness, the fear from the trees. The dead amongst 'em animating rage, because they remember what you hoped we'd forget.

You seen a revolt?

It looks like a carnival.

And Someone's dancing amongst them.

Io Evohe.

The Dead

On the Streets of Cities They Once Walked

"You guys mind if I pour some to dead?" he asked. A stranger. Homeless, on the stoop of a church.

His friend's aren't having it. It's a waste of beer. We're passers-by, lost in conversation. But I'm no longer surprised by this stuff.

"Hey–you guys don't mind, right?"

We turn. I smile. "Please do," I answer, and I feel them gathered. "Please."

Walk amongst the very poor, and you do not need good senses to know the dead are there. They talk about them, with them, to them.

On the streets you can hear them, in the shelters you hear them more, so many dead gathered together with so many living. They are all crammed together.

You need only listen, only watch the sideways glance of the old woman, the nod into air of the haggard veteran, the manic delight or panicked flight of the younger one just noticing: the dead don't go away.

Open yourself more and you hear bits of stories. Open further, and you cannot hear at all. The unremembered, unnoticed speak with a rage when you finally notice. More difficult still, they want the attention of others.

Where They May Be Found

On the street, the man looks at you and waves: joy of recognition, elation to see who he thought he'd never see again, someone he almost forgot. His mouth forms the name but his lips stop, quiver. Confused.

A shout from across the street. He starts to run but stops. You're not him. He's gone. You're not him.

When this first happens to you and then happens and happens you fear some cosmic joke, unfunny and sad.

But it's not you. It's Them, wanting to be seen.

When the Top-Hat Man's About

Guédé

Go searching and you'll find the stories. Children see him walk through their room, dead but really nice.

They aren't afraid. They shouldn't be.

The Haitians know him, and his kind and kin. Burning peppers and rum, a couple of hip-thrusts.

You might meet him under a tree, by the playground, like I did.

Now, he's on the edge of things. Close by those who've lost someone to despair.

There's the lover who found his best friend hanging in a closet. His best friend is still there, not in the closet but elsewhere, written all over his face, his fears, his sorrow. And the Guédé's nearby.

There's the stranger on the plane who stared at me. I was a bit afraid. "Ride back to Seattle?" he offered. This was dangerous, but I agreed. There was someone nearby. He found his roommate dead in the shower, veins opened and drained in the cascading torrent of chilling water.

He knows nothing of me, but he tells me all this and there's the man with the top-hat nearby.

And I still don't know why he's 'round the suicides most, 'round the friends they left behind.

In the Silences of Dry Words

Stories told by those who killed don't do much good to those they killed.

History is their voiceless litany. Dead Africans in hulls of ships, starved and sickened Natives hollowed by end of winter. Fingers broken on looms, eyes blinded by cinders, dust of coal in-breathed to make others rich. Massacres of miners who dared resist, forced marches and slaughtered children.

Your Face Is A Forest

Ropes hanging from trees, bombs dropped from planes, lead pumped through chest because they wouldn't say "yes."

These are the dead who scream, gathered in voiceless shouting to be remembered. Once you see the skeletons of the skyscrapers, they can't be unseen. So many sacrificed upon those altars, blood pouring in rivers to overflow our bank accounts.

They are in the leaves of books, the leaves of trees.

These are the dead we fear. They're waiting just on the other side, waiting to be heard.

Everywhere

We walk upon the dead. Fallen leaves, trees, dead birds, bugs, animals, dust from corpses, fecal remains from feast of crow and fang of beast.

The serene, enchanted forest is a charnel-house, the dazzling, powerful sea of stew of rotting bits swirling beneath sea-foam, feeding the living.

We are the living, composed of the dead. We eat the dead, arrayed in skin and hair of beasts, spun fibers of scythed grass and fur. We sweeten our drinks with the life-sap of slaughtered cane, inebriate our souls with pressed dead leaf, desiccated bean. John Barleycorn must die.

The dead inhabit our physical forms, giving us shape and life. We caress the dead skin of our lover's form, run our fingers playfully through tresses of dead hair, and this makes us feel more alive.

We burn the dead, distill them to make our fuels and plastics. The words I type are spun upon black liquid corpses of algae and plankton, the same you torch to drive your cars.

You cannot live without the dead.
You only live because of the dead.

And you and I will go with them.

Spirits of Land

Want to find land-spirits?

Get out of your car. Remove the roof, fill it full of soil, and plant a tree inside. Turn off your phone. If it's too smart to be turned off, apply open flame.

Pull out your headphones and smash them with a rock. Sweep up the pieces and dispose of them properly. If recycling facilities do not exist in your neighborhood, deposit the pieces on the desk of your local representative and request more public services.

Rip your television off the wall (gently, so to not destroy the plaster). Turn it face down in your bathtub and give it a nice, long, hot, relaxing bath. Add lavender and lilac petals to help ease the anxiety it's caused.

Or, mostly, just go for a walk.

Of Love & Land Spirits

We, by the Lake

Willow inclines her tasseled boughs towards the earth, but in the south, Oak is tasseled too, garlanded with Spanish Moss. Sage-blue tufts drape over branches, gossamer ribbons adorning the shade-queen of the summerlands. Willow mourns, but at night, so too does Oak, a dirging dance of stillness, unnoticed steps through silver light seeping through clouded skies.

A moon ago I sat under her cloaking branches with him, by the lake whose surface shimmered in slight breaths of wind. The moss swayed with that breath, but not with ours. Our voices, our fumbling mortal words barely disturbed the night, enveloped in the cooling air, smelling of late autumn's fecund slough and thick, humid flowerings.

I spoke, and then he spoke. Sometimes our words slipped over each other until our withdrawn silences overlapped–sudden ebb of sea from shore, wondering at apparent over-reach, eager to try again and again upon the patterns and pull of the moon. And yes–the moon was there. Everything was silver: his face, mine, the draping moss, the wax-green surface of leaf and grey-green skin of water, the white stone upon which we

Your Face Is A Forest

sat, the tree's dark roots silver-lined wooden slate.

We were not alone, though we were far from other mortals. And the moment we embraced, when our conversation became wordless and we remembered how to speak voicelessly, it was not just him, it was not just me. The moon behind and above him, the stone below, blue and green and grey of branch, silver of reflection, silver of star embraced us both.

She had seen, and smiled.

She, of the stream

I tended the spirit of a stream nearby this week. People throw so much trash into beautiful places I wonder if humans hate beauty, hate the spirits and gods for being not-us. Several bags of refuse (mostly plastic, that brilliant product of human "progress") extracted from the undergrowth along the stream's banks.

I tried to care for her with kindness, and children came out and sang Christmas carols as I scraped out cans and bottles from the base of fragile Elder and Plantain. A man with a dog passed by and thanked me, but all I felt from her was rage. I slipped and hurt my shoulder (badly) before giving her a libation of spring water from another land, and tried to reckon with her. I said to her, "we need you, even as we hurt you." I was very sore. "It's horrible, but maybe you can find your joy again. It's what I try to do, too."

They, of the three rivers

Three rivers meet and flow through the ancient city of Quimper in Bretagne. They didn't rage, but they were very forward. I didn't think they'd let me leave. Only after an oath to them did my pack lighten, my feet find purchase against cobbled street to meet an impending train and my next destination. "I'll try to return," I said. "And if I don't, I'll try to make a world where others will remember what you want and offer."

She, or maybe he, of the city

The two spirits I courted and co-created with in Seattle were more understanding. One, nearby, in a blind alley where people build tiny shrines understood fully. I met her, or maybe him, more Fae than anything else. I'd scrawled love notes on the walls by her home, love notes for a man who (like the man with me below the oak) became in the end a dream and memory of love. She'd seen those words. She understood why I'd leave.

Spirits of Land

She accepted my thanks, my endless gratitude for allowing me to co-create with her for so many years. And as I cried for the end of dreams and the closing of memories, she shook the leaves and branches of star-lit Birch.

He of the hillside and dying forest

A dear friend of mine has seen several of the spirits of the place he tends, where oak and alder rot from sudden-death. He's walked a hill in Northern California, seen marrow of tree suddenly gone soft, vast groves tumbled-down from whatever new thing we've done to this land. He drew a spirit as best he could. He'd found suddenly from his lungs erupt a First Nations' song he'd never heard, and later the spirit appeared, a Cyclops, raging against untimely, unexplained death. Raging against hillsides vanquished, lain bare and bald and naked to the warming climate.

Not everyone may be able to see them. Maybe some people cannot. Some people say we don't need to see them at all, or speaking of them this way is wrong. Some people even say they don't exist.

I think they do. I've seen them, or as best as I can so far. This is not just the province of the mystic or the seer, it is also the art of the Bard, who shows others not just how something can be seen, but that it exists both with and without us. This is the agency of the magician, this is how we world the earth.

A god appears to me and I say hello to him. A goddess laughs by a hearth in my dream and I seek her out. A spirit responds to my fumbling attempts at song, and I greet her and write about her and endure her ragings at what others have done to her. Sometimes they seem to have been waiting outside our consciousness our entire life, patiently wondering if we'd ever notice. And sometimes it is we who awaken them from their slumber.

There was a Welsh bard, Gwydion. Through his fumbling attempts to help his brother, he was cursed to run feral through the wilds with him, sire and be sired upon. And later, after a fumbling attempt to help his uncle, he came guardian of a goddess's son, awakening a mate for the child from oak and blossom. And this, too, did not turn out quite well.

There's a danger of being Gwydion. Spirits of land are not ours, even as we world them into our reckoning. They will not always love us. They may

Your Face Is A Forest

one day need to shake us off. But there is greater sorrow in not awakening them into our worldings–a world where they are trampled, ignored, forgotten, a world disenchanted.

I returned to that lake a few nights after to thank that spirit. Under the fullness of the moon I lit a candle I made, an offering of my own crafted light to warm the cold night, my exchange of love. And I saw her. And she told me to write about her.
And so I have.

What I Know Of A Creek

This morning, like most mornings, I rode my bike to work along a creek, my pockets stuffed with peanuts.

I've been feeding the crows, you see. My best friend does this, and taught me. He holds his hand in front of his face before tossing unsalted whole-shell peanuts where the corvids will see them. It'd been a practice I'd long intended to pick up, but I've only started it recently, and only after finding the corpse of a dead crow on one of my rides home from work.

The name of the one gods I worship, the most haunting presence of the five to whom I'm devoted, Brân, means "raven" in Welsh. He's also a god of Alder, and I'm still haunted by the time I saw a vision of him torn to pieces by ravens while straddling the valley of the River Aulne (Alder) in Bretagne.

And so I'm feeding crows along a stream, aware I'm not feeding ravens along a river, but I don't know how much this matters.

How men name rivers and streams (and its too often men, too often after themselves) in North America is rather ridiculous. It's like they don't actually ask the stream what it wants to be called.

Your Face Is A Forest

Men named this one Amazon Creek, supposedly on account of the sudden way it swells in the rains. On some maps, it's also called Amazon Slough. Eugene is surprisingly marshy; so much mud came with me into my home that I eventually relented a long-standing habit of not taking off my boots until I sleep. It takes a long time to unlace them, but it takes longer to scrub mud from carpet.

The water that doesn't soak the marshes rushes into the creek, when it doesn't rush into the rivers. Riding a bike in the rain is not always pleasant, but when it rains I know she'll be happy, and so I don't complain.

In other places I've lived, the creeks live under ground, traveling through pipes, fed by gutters, channeled far out of town into lakes or the sea. Creeks and streams aren't supposed to be in cities anymore–doesn't anyone remember the 1950s? Creeks are hazards–things live in them, grow in them. In the last century, they attempted to channel and reshape Amazon Creek. much like most of the last century brilliant men have been trying to drain the Everglades.

Bridges pass over it, the creek crawls under streets and, in many places, so does a path along it. I use this path to go to work, or to return from errands. Two weeks ago, I rode from a friend's house back to mine on the bike gifted by another friend, carrying on one shoulder an altar to Dionysos precisely the size and weight of a sturdy piano bench. (It was a piano bench before being an altar, and this is a brilliant idea.) A man with a dog stopped to applaud my balancing act, a young girl shouted in awe, asking "how are you doing that?"

There's graffiti along the path. Everywhere. A little over a year ago, I followed the path with a friend and found myself rooted to the ground, staring at a chalk drawing, a confluence of multiple vesica pisces sometimes called the Flower of Life, with the Kabbalistic Tree of Life chalked in a different color. I saw this figure again when I arrived in Seattle several months ago, moving blindly to Eugene. I left the airport for a cigarette, and it was the first thing I'd seen, chalked in the pavement by the benches in the smoker's area, and one more time upon finally arriving in Eugene. It's hard not to think this meant something.

I give offerings to the stream. The first time was a little weird. I stood over a bridge as homeless folk sat farther away in the grass, smoking marijuana. Perhaps to a stoner, a man pouring milk into a stream and muttering may seem no stranger than anything else people do, so I probably needn't have felt shy. The second time was in daylight, and it was impossible to hide what I was doing, but I am, after all, in Eugene, and the stream is beautiful.

The first few weeks here I was miserable. It rained. There was mud everywhere in my bedroom. I was poor and utterly uncertain what I was doing, terrified of not finding a job, wilting under bad florescent lighting in the home I share, very far from everything I knew. The first clear day I left the misery to walk along the stream, headed west, trudging for hours until I found myself in a wetlands as the sun began to set.

The next day I found a job. I'm not certain this is unrelated.

The creek is dirty. People throw things into it. Water washes away dirt and things you do not want upon your body; streams are lots of water, and they mostly do the same, except that we make lots of dirt so we can make money and then all of that dirt has to go somewhere, so it goes into the stream. There are shopping carts, dog toys, clothes, mattresses, fast food containers, a bike wheel. That's what I've seen.

I can't see the brake dust and exhaust particulate, or the motor-oil runoff, or the detergents or any of those other things we all need to create and need to get rid of because we have to be modern.

The creek is full of life, and not just the life we normally know. There are nymphs in several places, a spirit nearby under a tree who's looking for me. Someone's painted bizarre glyphs and sigils. Actually, several someones. They're of a system I don't comprehend, but it's not hard to sense that they've marked something they've seen.

It's not a creek, some've said. The waters start on the edge of a butte, and people want to build there because people want to be modern, I guess. If it's not a creek, then it's less important. Destroying a creek is different from destroying a place where water runs off, I guess. I don't understand.

I don't understand this creek, actually. I watch the birds in hopes they'll teach me something. Belted Kingfishers dart before me on the path and seem unconcerned whether I'll stop for them, because of course I will. Red-Winged Blackbirds haunt me to pieces. I got stared down today by a Great Blue Heron who didn't seem fully to approve of my attempts to photograph the stream. I couldn't move from where I stood, because I didn't feel I had permission.

Mostly, I just feed the crows. A few already know me. I suspect they know what I left on the spot where one of their family died. They dance before me on the path along the creek, ever closer. They seem to search me, to see if I'll ever learn the creek's name.

Under The Pavement, The Forest

I have a forest.

It's not mine, of course, anymore than anything else—my clothes, my home, my words—are mine or anyone's.

It's a forest. A small one, towering big-leaf Maples over small stands of Alder and scattered Cedars. A small stream bed, waiting for the relentless Seattle rains to fill its ravine with flowing life. Salmonberry is winning in its struggle with Blackberry, Snowberries with their understated leaves standing lightly over the sturdier Oregon Grape.

The Elder isn't quite supposed to be where it is, nor is the Hawthorn, but it is easy, once you've spent enough time by them, to understand why they're there, and I love them both. Even the Ivy, which has sadly choked from life to death a few of the younger Maples, has its charm and delight, for early-autumn Ivy blooms intoxicate as much as midsummer Jasmine and Nicotiana.

It's a forest, a small one, and it's mine, though it's no-one's, except its Self's. Following the paths between Fern and Fern, you find the small clearings, places to stand and dream, places to sit and think and sigh. And those particular places are where you find something else, something waiting.

Spirits of Land

I call them Gates, though this is no more a name for them than Hawthorn is for a tree, and perhaps less recognized. You may call them what you like, if you ever come visit. I hope one day you do, particularly when it's filled with candlelight.

These Gates are liminal places. It's the hollow beneath the tilted-lady Maple where something comes through or goes out; the small crevice of the velvet-moss covered fallen Cedar (wearing an Elder sapling like a feather) into which offerings are given and received. Places not easily gotten to, places none but those who are looking for something ever reach.

It's by one of these gates I see–well. I'd rather show you. Awfully playful, curious. Liked the stone I offered, but then gave it back. Too polished, I guess.

There was an Elk there. Or, no, not one living. There are no Elk nearby. Haven't been for decades, because cars are important now and they aren't. But an Elk played through there one night anyway, and the next day, the animals, painfully silent, finally returned. Its tooth, smeared with berries, left at a Gate.

It's not my forest, but I guess it's becoming my grove. And not just mine–I share it with a lover, and with friends, and with all those other Others who roam within its winding paths.

I love this forest. It's a short walk from my home, and is also part of my home. I live in a house on a hill in a city, a city I think I also love, but I think I'm in love more with what is barely noticed in the city than what it is known for, or what most people claim they see.

There's a term I first heard in Eugene, Oregon, posted on city arborist notices, the ones which proclaim the impending death of a tree because it's ruined the pavement or interferes with transmission lines. The term was "urban forest," and it was the first time I'd noted that others had a sense of what I'd sensed.

Next time you're outside, stare at the trees around you. In some places, it may take less effort than others, but look at those trees and see the forest that they are, how one tree connects to the next. Ignore the pavement and asphalt and buildings if you can, because they don't actually matter. This is the urban forest.

Unless you're awfully fortunate, you probably don't see enough trees. Probably, a road's in the way, or an office building or a parking lot. Imagine a forest underneath that pavement, waiting to come out. But cars need somewhere to drive, so we can't have a forest there.

Your Face Is A Forest

I'm awfully fortunate, as is my forest. It's a 'park,' owned by the city. Cars can't go through there, and no-one can build over it for now, so it's safe. The Gates where I leave offerings won't get smashed by bulldozers for a little while.

But I wonder about all the other Gates, the ones that might have been under the house I'm renting, or under the street I bike to get to work. How many more Gates to the Other were there and are gone now? How many more Alder, how many more Cedar? How many Elk?

Under that street is a stream. Actually, pipes, I guess, but a stream runs through it. A little bit of that stream empties into the lower part of my forest's stream before forced again below ground, out of sight.

There's a forest and a stream under my street! Which makes me want to rip up the pavement to get to it, because it seems quite awful that we would hide such things just so people can get to work fast.

I'm a bit…off, I guess. I've got wild ideas and never learned to make them go away. When I first understood we buried rivers under streets, I got awfully sad and then horribly angry. I'm still sad, and still angry, though not so sad and not so angry that I don't playfully follow their channels aboveground, tracing their paths under the city into the rivers and seas, dreaming.

I'm dreaming of those rivers returning, the forests returning, the Elk and Bison returning.

My forest is small, crowded with spirits and echos. It could be bigger. It should be bigger. But there are roads in the way…

…for now.

The Garments Of The Gods

We have our reasons when we travel. Work. Vacation. Friends and family and all the rituals of life and death with which we celebrate our existences and world our stories into each other. Sometimes wanderlust or curiosity, the need for refuge. Sometimes we flee a horrible place in hopes of security. Sometimes we travel towards a new place, one we do not yet know.

I don't know if we take our gods with us, or if they are always in everyplace, but I know they often look different. I wonder sometimes if Place is what clothes the gods in our presence. I met Brân in a grove of Alder in the Hoh Rainforest, just after playing music to ravens on an island. And I've met him elsewhere, in ritual, in prayers and devotions, but also in other places. Brân seen straddling a valley in Bretagne wore a cloak of ravens, but Brân further south wore black and red, or red and green and browns, Alder god amongst other Alders.

Dionysos in a gay bar wears less clothes than Dionysos in a grove, or in a certain grove in a certain vision. Dionysos furrowing the brow of a muscled ecstatic wears the face of a man, but at the pine tree shrine he wore the garments of earth. I like that he has many clothes.

Your Face Is A Forest

Arianrhod seen in the reflection of sky upon still clear water and Arianrhod seen in the wheeling of winter stars is familiar to me. But when I see Arianrhod in summer stars or the fading light off the shore of the sea, I know it is her, too. That she inhabits multiple dwellings and has a large wardrobe of many blues and silvers cheers me.

Where there are people, there are gods. Travel to one city far away from home and you see them, to another and they are there again, peering through different eyes, wearing foreign but beautiful raiment. Someone tells you about one you worship in a city of rain and hill, but they worship him at cave and in forest, and you hear his name and smile.

Where there aren't people, there are probably also gods, but I cannot know this, as I am people. There are certainly spirits when there are no people, but I do not know what they are up to when I am not looking. I do know each has so far been different, according to the place we met. The one by an ancient oak on a lake was different from the ones who played in the tassels of willow, and both different from the one in a street alley.

For the Christians, perhaps, it is also much like this. St. Catherine of the Wheel in one cathedral looks different from St. Catherine in a secluded chapel in another land, just as each church was forged of different stone, or different woods, and yet still a church. And she is both times St. Catherine.

I'm think on this whenever I travel, move in-between, staying in cities where I do not live until I come to the place where I live, having recently left a place where I, for awhile, lived. The places are different, but the gods were there, and are here, and have been everywhere I have yet been, wearing the land and people around them like beloved garments.

The Canticle Of The Gates

I'm hung-over, sipping tea, typing on a broken laptop balanced precariously upon a box of hand-written letters I've collected over the last 16 years. The screen is dirty: a thin layer of dust has settled upon all those things that are supposed to be kept dust-free, clean. It's not dust, or it is, but what is dust except old skin, lint, the thin layers of soil my boots track?

Actually, who am I kidding? It's incense ash, and it's everywhere. I smell like sandalwood and vetiver and bergamot, myrrh and gum benzoin and cedar, mugwort and damiana and cigarette smoke wherever I go. I inhale all this stuff into lungs, smear it over my face when my hand rubs my chin or massages my forehead in perplexity or unattended whim.

I'm hung-over, sipping tea, covered in incense ash, staring at a screen, trying to talk to you..

It's dim. I can't see well when it's bright—the sun reveals too much, image overload, my eyes drowning in sight.

It's dim, it's overcast, and the play of light and shadow upon my hands as I watch myself type are subtle, cautious, toned in the illumination of thought and dream. Dust and ash and cold tea and greys and greens outside my window battling against the electric blues of this screen, beckoning

Your Face Is A Forest

me to explore past it into the play of backlit-life, the dance of images and imaginings but nothing imaginal, only symbol.

I stood on the banks of a canal and watched a gate open in the rhythmic disruption of refraction and reflection, October sun screeching mechanically against the surface of the sluggish water whipped by wind. Follow it, go just past it, and you can find Arianrhod, which is an awfully strange thing to say.

I've lit more incense. You should get more tea. You're going to need it for this.

I do.

To tell you what I've seen, I use words. Words are full of meaning, meaning corresponds with sound that you conjure in your head as your eyes scan across this page, decoding and inhabiting the lines, shapes, and spaces of black on white. I cannot show you my world, how I expelled everything from my stomach repeatedly last night, naked on a bathroom floor thinking of The Mothers and how really strange it that I not only cannot eat seafood, but I can't swallow a guy who recently did.

I ran to the sea the other day, fast. I had to. Someone was calling. It was Him, or one of those Hims, he with a name, he I didn't know until I knew. It's cold, raining, and I want to take off my clothes and run into his domain, find one of his Gates, but instead I just unwittingly shout "father" and "thank you."

I can't eat what comes from the sea, unlike every other member of my family. It seems a bit of cannibalism.

Trees are of the sea, and the trees closest to rivers make the most sense to me. Willow and Alder clinging to stream banks, overhanging—they are the easiest gates, though Yew with its roots trying the worm-eaten corpse and Elder whose hidden foundation touches even further down where none of us should go--both willing doors.

Just prop it open as you enter.

Trees aren't of the sea, I know. Except we all are. They, pillars of water, sheathed in bark and wood, dancing on winds as they feed on the blackened wet death below the forest floor—they, more than anyone, know that we've forgotten how to enter.

Spirits of Land

In the shadowlands, that dim space lit with no sun at all, the shores glisten and sparkle between sea and forest. There are caves there, and stars, and long ribbons of stone-dust rimed with salt. There's a gate there, and a bridge without guard-rails, and you can fall off into water or land and be lost to the other for a little while.

The point is to stay-between.
The point is always to stay in-between. Between dream and waking, sobriety and ecstasy, life and death, embody them both without taking a side. But that's no point at all, but a path, and it leads into the place which is nowhere and about-to-be-everywhere.

It's exhausting. How's your tea?

A lover and I dreamt the same dream of the world-between-the-walls. Everything in that city was full, too full and there was nowhere to breathe, nowhere to sleep, nowhere. Others came and went, and we didn't know where they came from, because there was no space for them, no space for us.
They lived in the walls. Between their space and no-space was another space, vast, endless, and invisible. Unseen unless you entered, but you could not enter unless you left the crowded, thronging, suffocating world where we all live.
To enter, you needed to find a Gate.

You stop looking for the patterns which open them, because it's painful to know that they're everywhere and you're not going in. I mean, you have to go to work, and make dinner, and there's a movie you want to watch, and you have to make a decision.
To know the dead are everywhere, and the gods, and not to be looking at them—that's a strange thing, like ignoring your lover's body, glistening with sweat on a warm day, beckoning you towards it but, well, you wanted to check email.
Filtering them out (a screen is a filter) keeps you 'sane' and balanced, but also is awful. You have to do it, or you want to do it, because you cannot possibly live your life constantly in rapture or ecstasy or wonder. You've got bills to pay. You've got to eat, man.
Humans "cannot bear very much reality," said a bird in a poem by a poet I'm not allowed to quote here. And what could a bird really know of

Your Face Is A Forest

this, what it's like for us, what we can and cannot see? It doesn't do stuff it doesn't want to do in order to pay rent in a place one doesn't necessarily really want to live but it's cheaper than what you want so you live there.

Mostly, I suspect, we just get in its way, like we get in the way of trees and streams, and it tolerates us, perhaps laughs at us, and mostly hopes we figure it out, or leave it alone.

But we filter out that bird, and the trees. We bury the streams under pavements, the forests under highways, we block out the sea with great tall buildings which are walls without gates, huddling together, all waiting to fall.

I've gotten more tea. I'm still hung over, trying to tell you about Gates, how to get in, which is also how to get out.

In some traditions, the ritual circle has "gates," gates according to the directions. At the Gate of Beltane, I saw the cliffs we jump off of, back into the sea. Sense what's not there and you want to flee, running headlong into madness or delirium. We cannot bear very much reality, and there's always a way out that isn't through. Walk through the gate and you get stopped. You can't just go on, not 'till you figure out what you're running from. At the Solstice of Summer, the sky fell away, the sun shone as another star. Do you know what's behind the sun?

Nothing. And stare at it long enough and it spins and goes black and opens a gate.

I don't like what I've seen at Lughnasadh, or Samhain, or Imbolc. I don't like what the gods show you when you enter through. I don't like seeing what we're all about to do to ourselves, and the horrible things we've already done, the reason why they've fled from us, receded into that sea, walking backwards, waiting, hoping some of us get it right.

Here is a gate, and here is another gate. There are the gates that go out, and the ones which go in.

Remember that time you could not stop looking at a tree? Some slant of gold and rose light through its leaves and you couldn't look away though you had elsewhere to go, otherwise to do?

Remember that feeling, sublime loss of self, unbidden rapture? There was a gate there, and someone was guarding it.

That time the sea threatened to drown you as you stood at the shore, her or his or its thunder coursing now also in your veins, shaking, quaking all

Spirits of Land

which tethers bone to muscle to skin? You stood at a Gate, looking in, and They looked out.

In Nature, the gates are everywhere, raw life shattering as it gets closer to the edge of what we are and what we cannot be any longer.

The polluted stream under the bridge you drive over daily to get to work, the one you look away from every time, the one you stop noticing? Go look, and ask yourself why you looked away in the first place.

The alley you pass by, cluttered with fallen autumnal leaves, wet with puddles, isolated, lonely, the rain falling slant against old brick. The alley you pass by and glance into and it shapes your thoughts, changes for a moment the threaded pattern of anxious wonderings and stressed frustration. Walk down it.

Your dog barks at nothing, the cat bolts into the thin air, your child is certain something is there you just can't see it and they want you to explain but you can't. The woman on the bus speaks to no-one, shaking her head with laughter you really can't bear to hear.

Not every voice is in our head, but many of them are: the advertisements, the jingles, the boss's scolding because you will be late, your mother's judgment or your neighbor's prattling. The lost lover's whisper, the dead friend's laughter. Echoes, recollections, fragments you encounter then forget, then remember, then forget.

Not every voice in our head, but the ones from elsewhere don't shout with voice.

They come through the gates to greet us, they flee through the gates at our approach.

We are so loud, our cars music jackhammers fights and laughter, our stereos which surround, our engines which rumble past what needs silence to sing. We shout at nothing, a screen across which men run across false-grass. We thumb and touch and stare at the smaller screens, white tendrils clinging close to the tympani of our skull.

In these images, these frames, there can be nothing else but what we are shown. Not gates but tableaux, processions of shadows from which we weave meaning. She? She was shot. See? This kitten has had a bad day.

What are you looking at? We say to the mad, or the child, or pet, or the poet.

Everything else, they could say, but we can't hear them.

Your Face Is A Forest

That desert prophet asked how we can love what we haven't seen when we do not love what we have.

We travel far to find something to see, to love. Drives into mountains, planes to sun-strewn shores and ancient stone walls. We travel so far, over sea through air or across razed forests and dead buffalo sealed-over with asphalt to make our roads.
Or we bask in blue light, searching. This land here has a mystery, this hotel there serves good breakfast. See? The narrow warrens of this crowded city, cobbled, smell of spice, this mountain is taller than others you've seen and is cold at the top. Look what they had for dinner.
See? Life is elsewhere, the magic drained from our dredged swamps and extracted from our flattened mountains. See? Other lands bear magic still for us and take Visa and speak English.

I've walked through cities with gates, great tors and stone towers, small arched openings in crumbling sandstone or brick. There's plenty magic there for them, enough almost to share. But those aren't the Gates they see, nor the Gates through which They come.
Walk drunk through city streets in the rain and stop, suddenly broken, suddenly broken—look! Something older than you, something older than everything you've seen.
The streets in those place whisper, this is a good place to live. A myriad of souls have walked these stones before, woke, worked, fucked, laughed, lived, died. A myriad of souls have seen the gates, walked through them or crossed themselves as they passed.
But under our streets still decompose flesh bone wood and fur, and we think that we are different.

It's gets dark sometimes. Out of the Gates pour what we ignore, what we cannot become, what we will not admit. The rivers of blood, the mass graves, the slow deaths and felled forests all drain back in, seep away into an ocean we will not allow to be real.
But the bulldozers and explosives don't remove the mountain, they displace it; the rivers flow under our streets, the forests spring up through the pavement. That black blood in subterranean wells doesn't go away when it burns.

The gates don't always close from our side.

Spirits of Land

Sometimes all the sound around you makes another sound, and a song comes through.
Sometimes the babble of strangers conspires in concert to tell you something.
Sometimes everything we do to wall them out becomes their path back in.
Sometimes.

I'm mostly trying to open the Gates that are closed, find the ones hidden, but it's for nothing if we don't enter.

A shrine marks the path in, a fountain the path out. Here, a well; here, a cave.
What stands there, waiting, guarding, cannot be ignored, anymore than we can be ignored.
Strewn trash in a stream, shopping center on a cemetery, whirring cars and suffocating cement.
Invite them back to a cluttered, dirty house. Come in, here, ignore the smell, the rot, the plastic and paper upon the chairs, fast food wrappers and cereal boxes on the table, the loud television and let me check my phone for a moment.

The gates most often close from our side.

Between the walls, between the worlds, in shimmering dance of light in leaf, rippled refraction on river, there is space for them, space for us.

The rest is opening the Gates

And going through.

GODS&RADICALS PRESS
is a not-for-profit Pagan anti-capitalist publisher.
For more information about our works, visit our websites:
ABEAUTIFULRESISTANCE.ORG
GODSANDRADICALS.ORG

www.ingramcontent.com/pod-product-compliance
Lightning Source LLC
Chambersburg PA
CBHW070430010526
44118CB00014B/1976